Faith and the Prospects of Economic Collapse

FAITH
and the
PROSPECTS
of
ECONOMIC
COLLAPSE

ROBERT LEE

John Knox Press
ATLANTA

Library of Congress Cataloging in Publication Data

Lee, Robert.
   Faith and the prospects of economic collapse.

   Bibliography: p.
   Includes index.
   I. Christianity and economics.   2. Christianity
and justice.   3. United States—Economic conditions
—1971–   I. Title.
BR115.E3L37   261.8′5   80–82187
ISBN 0–8042–0814–X (pbk.)

© copyright 1981 John Knox Press
10 9 8 7 6 5 4 3 2 1
Printed in the United States of America
John Knox Press
Atlanta, Georgia 30365

OTHER BOOKS by Robert Lee

The Social Sources of Church Unity—Selected for the Kennedy White House Library (Abingdon)

Cities and Churches, Editor (Westminster)

Protestant Churches in the Brooklyn Heights (New York Protestant Council)

Religion and Social Conflict, Editor with Martin Marty (Oxford University Press)

Religion and Leisure in America (Abingdon)

The Churches and the Exploding Metropolis, Editor (John Knox Press)

Directory of Centers for the Study of Society (Towne House Publishers)

Stranger in the Land: A Study of the Church in Japan (Lutterworth); (Friendship)

The Schizophrenic Church (Westminster)

The Promise of Bennett (Lippincott)

The Spouse Gap, with Marjorie Casebier (Abingdon); (Collins); (Friedrich Bahn Verlag Konstanz)

Marriage Enrichment Sharing Sessions (Minister's Life Resources)

China Journal: Glimpses of a Nation in Transition (East West Publishing)

CONTRIBUTING AUTHOR

The Church and Its Changing Ministry (General Assembly, United Presbyterian Church)

The Dilemma of Organizational Society (E.P. Dutton)

Evangelism and Contemporary Issues (Tidings)

The Challenge to Reunion (McGraw-Hill)

Heirlooms (Harper and Row)

Dictionary of Christian Ethics (Westminster Press)

Masterpieces of Christian Literature (Salem Press)

Ethics and Bigness (Harper and Brothers)

Preaching on National Holidays (Fortress Press)

The Church and Urban Renewal (Lippincott)

Life and Mission of the Church (National Student Christian Federation)

Christianisme Social (Cooperative d'editions et de Publications, Paris)

Contents

Preface

The amber lights of warning are now blinking. If we continue on our present course, they will be followed by the red lights of disaster!

Well-meaning and concerned people are suddenly bewildered and confused, as they read about the loss of confidence in the once mighty American dollar. General awareness is dawning that this loss of confidence is undermining the industrial economies in the Western world, creating monetary instability, contributing to soaring inflation rates, and precipitating a runaway explosion in commodity prices—particularly gold and silver. Panic buying and selling, with wild price fluctuations in these precious metals, is itself a warning signal of danger ahead.

This book is an effort to help people of good will understand better the complex issues of our economy. It initiates a dialogue of what a Christian response might be to issues that have for too long been ignored or disdained by religious believers, who resent the intrusion of material matters upon their spiritual vision.

Although many of the economic realities discussed in these pages appear gloomy, the book concludes on an upbeat note that calls for repentance and a change in our life style. Books that feature economic gloom and doom are gaining in popularity. The Christian message, however, is not simply one of doom; it also proclaims salvation. It is Good News for those who seek the bread of life. It is a message of love and compassion.

For those with eyes of faith, the biblical note of judgment does not end in hopelessness and despair. It culminates in newness of life, a restoration of faith and confidence. This vision is affirmed in the Book of Revelation: " 'Behold, I make all things new.' " (Rev. 21:5)

In addition to confronting the issues of inflation and the declining rate of productivity, this book centers on a diagnosis of the virulent debt disease that afflicts many American institutions, corporations, banks, municipalities, and individuals, who have become consumer "creditholics."

It may seem incongruous for a student of theology and ethics to be writing about economic matters pertaining to money and credit. Yet I feel this work stands in the tradition of the prophet who is warning a profligate people about their collision course with calamity.

Americans face a severe time of testing during the early years of the 1980s. Many are whistling in the dark while walking through the graveyard, casting a wary glance over their shoulders, and reassuring themselves that nothing can really go wrong. Who wants to think the unthinkable? Despite disturbing economic facts, it is more comforting to assume that the government and the economists have everything under control.

We have grown accustomed to periodic recessions that, since the sixties, have recurred in roughly four-year cycles. But the prospects of a serious depression?

"Never! At least not in my lifetime," goes the popular sentiment.

It is quite possible, however, that the imbalances and distortions run so deep in our economic structure that only a massive upheaval of debt liquidation can correct the cumulative abuses that have been building up over the past three decades. The prospect of economic collapse is not simply confined to the American domestic scene, for the problem is global and systemic.

No easy answers are available. As in the case of an earthquake, one may make preparations and take precautionary steps, but one cannot prevent it from happening in its own moment of ripeness when sufficient subterranean pressures have built up.

Our American proclivity is to look for simple solutions—

gimmicky, "how-to" techniques, especially the individualistic, survival-kit type—without even pausing to understand the dimensions of the problem. I hope the reader will resist this impulse, which is examined in the final chapter with a critique of the doomsday prescriptions of Howard Ruff and Harry Browne. Such prescriptions are merely instances of ego-ethics in the face of a structural, systemic crisis that calls for communal response or eco-ethics.

Here is my prophetic warning in a nutshell: The economy is vulnerable to collapse on a scale comparable to the 1930s. Most people already feel that something is wrong when they face the everyday realities of double-digit inflation or when they seek to purchase a home at ridiculously inflated prices. Inflationary growth, which is fueled by expansive credit, cannot be sustained indefinitely and will buckle when *confidence* falters. Confidence, or public faith, is the binding force of our economy and our financial system. The greater the inflationary pressures, the more vulnerable we are to the coming trauma in public confidence. When public confidence subsides, the economy will collapse.

Warning signals of impending collapse are developed in various chapters, which I shall now highlight for the reader who wishes to skip around.

Chapter I on "The Credit Binge and Economic Collapse" examines the explosion in consumer credit and the role of credit cards, which are discussed as plastic power and plastic perils.

Chapter II explores the banking system's addition of fuel to the credit fire. Banks are not simply managers of depositors' assets but have become money-creating machines through the practice of borrowing short and lending long.

Chapter III probes the role of the federal government as the chief architect of the debt pyramid and gatekeeper of the money supply. The national debt, government spending, and the meaning of money are also analyzed.

Chapter IV examines some tragic "Unlearned Lessons from History" in the runaway inflation and credit binges of Germany,

France, and the Great Depression. Those who are convinced that "it can't happen here again" would do well to study the past in the light of present-day excesses. This chapter also contains a provocative caveat about religious depressions preceding economic crises.

Chapter V discusses "Bankruptcy and the American Way of Debt." One of the painful consequences of the overextension of credit is the trip to the bankruptcy court. Widespread bankruptcies will mark the period of economic collapse. Even during the "recovery" years of 1976–79, more than 600 American families declared bankruptcy every day. People of faith need to be alert to the grief and poignancy of the bankruptcy experience.

Inflation would not pose its clear and present danger were it accompanied by rising productivity. Alas, such is not the case. One key factor in the lagging rate of American productivity is the decline of the traditional work ethic. Hence Chapter VI, "Whither the Work Ethic: Rehumanizing Work," analyzes what has happened to the Protestant-Puritan work ethic and how the movement toward rehumanization of work can stem the tide of worker disenchantment and thereby contribute to increased productivity.

The final chapter, "Econ-fidence: Faith and Economics," expounds on the dialogical and even symbiotic relationship between faith and economics. Chapter VII reiterates the theme that faith, or public confidence, is the force that sustains the economy, particularly its debt and credit system. This last chapter advances a new and rather startling interpretation of Proposition 13 as an important mythic symbol of our time. It calls for a shift from ego-ethics to eco-ethics—a simple living pledge involving care, concern, and commitment—and concludes on a note of judgment and hope for the restoration of confidence.

One final preliminary word is in order. As a professor of ethics and theology, I am concerned about economic issues—excessive debt, inflation, consumerism, profligacy, and the prospects of economic collapse—not because of any antiquated nostalgia for a return to Protestant-Puritan ethics. I seek not to lament the passing of a tradition or to pine for the good old days and the good old ways (which always turn out never to have been that good). Nor do I intend to lob moral stones at glass houses. My intent is to relate the concerns of faith to the issues of our economy. If I sense danger ahead, I am not alone, but stand with a cloud of witnesses in good company. The highly respected periodical *Bank Credit Analyst* concluded a lengthy analysis of our inflated credit economy with these words of warning:

> The financial system has become increasingly out of joint with the real part of the economy. Such a disequilibrium means that the financial system, if abused, will become, as it has in previous cycles, too unstable to support sustained prosperity. The financial system is always the Achilles' heel of any program of forced growth, and this is particularly true of the environment which exists today, as it is highly prone to inflation and debt problems.[1]

My concern for economic issues was first aroused by Kenneth Underwood while he was teaching social ethics at Yale Divinity School in the mid-fifties. His premature death robbed the field of one of its ablest minds. Ken used to argue that a change in the discount rate or in the prime rate ought to be of major concern to ethicists because it had repercussions in social policy and decision making and, thus, had an important impact on human life and destiny.

My hope is that the reader will not be bogged down by the grim statistics and facts that are necessary if the dialogue between faith and economics is to be fruitful. Indeed, the study of social ethics is a dialogue between faith and facts.

Several readers of the manuscript have expressed surprise at the critical stance I have taken toward the fraternity of establishment economists. No less a figure than a recent Secretary of the Treasury has expressed similar skepticism about our expert economists:

> Reliable sources are no longer reliable. Those wonderfully complicated mathematical models of the economy have turned treacherous. They offer as many false leads as cor-

rect ones. The experts who know most about the economy now have the least certainty about it. The traditional crystal balls have been reduced to ground glass. Those who are most emphatic in their judgments and prognostications are almost without exception touched with arrogance and blessed with ignorance. Wisdom speaks in terms that are grey, hedged, unquotable.

Note that shortly after this speech to the New York Financial Writers Association in the summer of 1979, Secretary Michael Blumenthal was abruptly dismissed from his post.

Readers will find that this volume raises many questions, some of which are deeply disturbing. It challenges many of our fundamental assumptions and cherished values, which we have taken so much for granted as necessary to our way of life. As a warning signal, this book is more concerned with raising the issues of collapsing confidence and the overextension of debt and credit *while there is still time to do so* than with finding easy and immediate solutions. My concern is for truth-telling in an effort to approximate the wisdom contained in these thoughtful lines written by Sir Thomas Browne in 1620:

> *Some have keen wits to know the truth.*
> *Some have strong hearts to tell the truth.*
> *But how few know to tell it so*
> *That all may see it is the truth.*

I wish to acknowledge my indebtedness and gratitude to many people whose support and encouragement have made this volume possible: President Arnold Come, trustees, and colleagues at San Francisco Theological Seminary, for granting me a sabbatical leave; President Everett Kleinjans, whose invitation to serve as Senior Fellow at the East-West Center in Honolulu enabled my early reflections on the subject; President Bill Pinson of Golden Gate Baptist Seminary, for his friendly and helpful counsel; and James Whelpley, for his intellectual prodding and stimulus. Various readers of the manuscript have offered valuable critiques: Browne Barr, John C. Bennett, Robert Coote, Robert de Fremery, Eric Haessler, and Howard Rice.

My hosts at various places have provided generous hospitality plus an audience for reaction: Dr. Carl Nissen and the Magnolia Ministerial Association in Seattle, Washington, for the Howard Lavelle Lectures; Dr. Darrel Berg of Rockbrook United Methodist Church and Dr. Vernon Goff of St. Luke's Methodist Church in Omaha, Nebraska; Dr. Ron Lundeen and the congregation at Advent Lutheran Church in Des Moines, Iowa; Dr. James Emerson and Dr. John Evans of Calvary Presbyterian Church in San Francisco; and the Reverend Oakley Dyer, who served as host during the Pastoral Institute Lectures in Calgary, Canada.

My wife, May, has been a constant source of strength and would be my nominee for sainthood; and my children Mellanie, Marcus, Matthew, Wendy, and Michele Miko have shared our pilgrimage in memorable ways.

R.L.
San Anselmo, California

I

The Credit Binge and the Prospects of Economic Collapse

Inflation, Stagflation, Deflation, Recession, Rolling Readjustment, Contraction, Banana. Call it what you will, there is a general malaise about economic matters, a feeling of *dis-ease* that is gaining like a ground swell in the American public. Despite higher incomes and the appearance of prosperity, countless people are having trouble making ends meet. They read disturbing headlines about the sagging, sinking, staggering dollar and the stagnant economy. They sense that the "Almighty Dollar" has fallen, and that the time-honored phrase, "as sound as a dollar," has a hollow, hyperbolic ring to it nowadays.

Increasingly the American public has lost confidence in the ability of its governmental leaders to "manage the economy." Confidence is fast dwindling also in economists, for despite their technical talk and computerized printouts, their record of forecasting has been as dismal as their discipline. Both governmental advisors and private economists set forth a confusing array of conflicting data—the latter are a tower of babel, a veritable cacophony of voices from fine-tuners to free-market noninterventionists, while the former are forever issuing denials, revisions, and surprises.

Ebullient talk of abundance, unlimited growth, an affluent society has given way to concern about limits and depletable resources, and grave doubts as to whether or not any national leader in Washington can pull us through the economic turbulance. Where there was once an air of optimism, a hopeful sense of progress, an American utopian outlook, there is now a growing sense of impending doom and the fear that hard times lie ahead and that things will move from bad to worse. Pessimism rides high in the saddle, and confidence is at the straining point. People sense a failure of nerve on the part of leaders, touching off thereby the nerve of failure in the body politic.

In the old days of euphoria, growth was our friend, producing not just a larger slice of the pie, but a larger pie itself, or even many pies—and cake too. With unlimited growth, we had an unending banquet table to which the rest of the world was invited to share our surplus (or our crumbs), thanks to Almighty Growth.

Now the tables are turned. In the new days of despair, growth has become our enemy. Unrestrained growth is raping our land, fouling our air, ruining our streams and rivers, outstripping our food bins, bringing "artery sclerosis" to our cities, and depleting our natural resources.

Rational thinkers are warning that things may have gotten out of hand, that we are in a runaway society, careening madly toward oblivion. Stop growth! Put on the brakes! Cut it back! Beware the 25th hour—which is the hour after the 24th. Thus Robert Heilbroner's *Inquiry into the Human Prospect* suggests that the feeling of dismay, bordering on despair, is due in part to the sobering realization that rationality has its limits with regard to the engineering of social change. That is, problems won't be solved simply through growth, or by throwing enough money at them, as the erudite John Kenneth Galbraith once proposed. "One of these unmanageable events," writes Heilbroner, "is the apparently unstoppable inflation that we witness in every industrialized capitalist nation."[2] Heilbroner depicts America as going through the dark night of the soul, moving through a long, dark tunnel with no light yet visible at the end. Times will get much worse before any light can be glimpsed. In a similar mood, another pessimistic prognosis is offered by Robert A. Nisbet: "If one were to wager, we should expect a few decades of drift toward military leviathanism set in conditions of social erosion and cultural decay."[3]

We are being given many danger signals that warn of a coming collapse. The amber light that blinks clearest to my limited vision is the credit binge, the overextension and excesses of credit and debt at all levels of spending.

Let me be clear at the outset that I am not inveighing against credit *per se,* only its excesses and abuses. It is obvious that credit is the lubricant of our production, distribution, and consumption system. Credit is the very woof and warp of the fabric of modern commerce. Hardly a venture is undertaken, from the building of a house to the development of solar energy, without the stimulus of credit. Even mighty IBM, that citadel of corporate liquidity, has gone to the debt market to raise an additional $1.5 billion in bank credit and $1 billion in debentures and bonds to undergird its new generation of computers. We are speaking of excessive and inordinate overextension of credit, of an unrestrained appetite for credit, of being drowned in a sea of credit—bearing in mind, to shift the metaphor, that too much debt incurred is like a cork that is easy to float but exceedingly difficult to sink.

Note that our word "credit" comes from the Latin *credo.* It originally referred to faith and fidelity and trust. Our words "credence" and "credibility" come from the same root. Thus, credit implies that the lender trusts the debtor and believes in his or her ability to repay. *Credo,* or creed, also means a belief system or a set of dearly held convictions. Those who have hopelessly overextended their credit and are unable to repay are beyond belief in more ways than one. Note further the euphemism, which sounds more elegant, that one has a "line of credit" at the bank, rather than confessing that one is in debt to the bank. One can "enjoy" credit but mourn about debt; yet they are one and the same.

So many people—ranging across all ages, income levels, and social classes—spend up to and even beyond their incomes, until they are in hock up to their eyeballs.

Item: Here is the case of a prominent surgeon, enjoying a $150,000 yearly income, and yet nearly flat broke after 15 years of medical practice. He pays alimony to two ex-wives, sustains a life style that includes a yacht and a boat, a heavily mortgaged $650,000 home, a 280 SEL Mercedes-Benz, and a 924 Porsche, and indulges a proclivity for fine wines and for frequenting gambling casinos.

Item: Here is a young couple, living in St. Paul, Minnesota, who began their marriage with $2,500 in joint debts. They went right on spending. After two years their debt climbed to $13,000. They had bought a stove, freezer, refrigerator, washer and dryer, and a house full of furniture—all on installment credit. More credit was assumed for a car and new clothing for work. Then came a $40,000 mortgage on a home. The wife became pregnant and left her job. Unanticipated medical bills, repairs on the car, and higher-than-expected fuel bills piled up alongside their other charges. Result: bankruptcy.

Item: Here is a single parent, living in the ghetto area of Oakland, California, and trying to support three children on her $7,000 income as a clerk. After paying the rent, the day-care center, clothing costs, and grocery and medical bills, there is simply not enough left over to pay installment charges for the color television, the new car, household furnishings, and assorted credit card charges.

Those who yearn to possess everything they see and everything they hear that others possess will likely become debtors —particularly if lending institutions (banks, credit unions, finance companies) avidly ply their trade by extending credit at interest. Money, of course, is the product that these financial institutions are coaxing the public to buy.

My thesis is that the issues of inflation, recession, depression, debt, and credit are not just economic issues. They are also moral and theological issues. They profoundly affect human lives and destinies, hopes and fears, and raise both domestic and global ethical issues.

My further contention is that confidence is the cement that holds together our entire economic house of cards. Confidence is the litmus test for any meaningful money system. In the middle of that word confidence is *fides,* the Latin term for faith. Indeed, the dictionary definition of faith is "a confident belief in the truth, value, or trustworthiness of a person, idea, or thing." Some other commonly used terms that emanate from *fides* are fidelity, fiduciary, and even federal. Later in this volume we will examine how faith or confidence in the *federal* government and in the *Federal* Reserve System is critical for monetary reassurance. Confidence is the support system of our economy. Without confidence, there is the danger of fear and panic.

Without going too far afield, let us explore the role of confidence in everyday economic relations. Confidence is the key to understanding economic transactions between two or more parties, such as buyer-seller, tenant-landlord, employer-employee. Economic life consists of countless thousands of exchanges which are honored in the overwhelming majority of cases. Confidence rules these relationships in the tacit understanding that both parties will fulfill their obligations. Their common expectations are built on confidence that has been reasonably and repeatedly justified in previous encounters. Thus, if a shopper selects a cart full of groceries at the supermarket, the merchant generally has confidence that the groceries will be wheeled to the check-out stand and paid for. It is confidently assumed that the hungry diner who orders items from a menu at a restaurant will pay the bill. In exchange for living in rental property, the confident assumption is that the tenant will pay the landlord. The employee has confidence that his work will be rewarded with payment by the employer.

If payments are made in cash in these transactions, the exchange is consummated immediately, and the confidence is justified on a very short-term basis. Note, however, that our economic relations have become highly complex, and cash payments are becoming more rare. Indeed, some would say we have entered the era of the "cashless society." Increasingly our transactions are not completed ones. Instead, debt is incurred with a promise to pay later. Exchanges are deferred—as in installment-buying plans and real-estate mortgages. Confidence is all the more necessary over a long-term basis, because confidence in the promise to pay at a future date makes possible the extension of credit. Like a finely spun web, confidence extends throughout the economic system. Once the web weakens or is broken, the whole system is vulnerable to collapse.

Public confidence, of course, can be fickle, like the sudden shifts of a summer storm. Even the students of mass behavior and crowd psychology have difficulty fathoming the public mood with its herd responses. Who knows how confidence is elusively gained and then abruptly broken, whether it is justified by the facts or is as inexplicable as the assassin's bullet that cuts down a popular leader? Who knows how charisma is won and lost or how yesterday's cultural heroes can become today's goats?

Like conscience, confidence exists behind the green doors in the secret chambers of the individual. It is not amenable to coercion or deception. Yet in its public expression, it can respond to mass hysteria in mercurial ways. It is pregnable to shock.

Although we are speaking of public confidence as a mood response, which is elusive and difficult to pinpoint, empirical surveys do exist to measure the public's confidence in political leaders and purchasing plans, and the public's feelings of economic well-being. Albert Sindlinger has devised a frequently cited Consumer Confidence Index. Likewise, the University of Michigan at Ann Arbor conducts a Consumer Confidence Survey of households, which, as of August 1979, reached a record low of 64, down 14 points from the previous year's figures.

Periodic reports on business confidence are issued by the Conference Board based on a nationwide survey of 1,600 chief executives of corporations. In September 1979, the board's study indicated a steady decline in business confidence to a low of 32, a decline from 41 in June 1979 and from 49 in September 1978.

We are at a crucial time, when public confidence is being tested by the moral dimensions of economic issues. Surely inflation is a moral issue. It robs people on fixed incomes and low incomes—the elderly, pensioners, and the poor. Inflation is immoral in the classical, prophetic sense, because it hurts most those who can least afford it. Its victims are found among the defenseless, those with little voice or power to protest or to fight back. Those who are the most financially vulnerable must suffer not only inflation's high costs, but also the restraints of the subsequent recession. And as we will examine in chapter IV the more rampant the inflation, the deeper the recession that follows.

Inflation saps the morale of a people and turns the cheerful into cynics. A thrifty person who has saved funds for retirement, hoping to watch the assets grow as interest is compounded, now suddenly discovers the penalty: the money has dwindled drastically in purchasing power. No wonder an elderly widow sadly pins a lapel button on her congressional representative with the message: "Savings may be hazardous to your wealth." While the saver is punished, Uncle Sam comes to the aid of the borrower with a tax deduction for the interest paid.

Inflation erodes purchasing power, cheats savers, and discourages the traditional virtue of thrift. Instead, it encourages spending, rewards profligacy, raises wage demands on the part of unions anticipating higher prices, and pushes up prices by businesses expecting higher costs or price controls. Inflation wreaks havoc on people and corporations alike. Individuals find their hard-earned savings evaporating, while corporations find future planning virtually impossible. Inflation strains credibility and morale and ultimately shatters confidence.

Inflation is a moral issue, moreover, because of the illusions it perpetrates: the illusion of greater income and wealth, when purchasing power is actually less; the illusion that one can spend now and worry later (or not at all); and the illusion that government will manage the economy by spending as much as is necessary to solve problems, when such problems are intractable and simply not that amenable to expedient solutions. In a sense, the greatest immorality is living by illusions. In the end, deception provides false premises for human decision making.

I contend that easy and excessive credit fuels inflation. In turn, inflation adds to the demand for credit and stimulates more rapid growth of debt. Despite the Apostle Paul's admonition to avoid getting into debt, except the debt of mutual love (Rom. 13:8), we have become a nation of creditholics—carefree and prodigal spenders who are drunk with credit. Creditholism is a present-day addiction not unlike being hooked on drugs or alcohol. It is the same irresistible and irrepressible urge which knows no boundaries, which goes to excess by escaping into a buying binge.

By the fall of 1979, total consumer debt outstanding, including home mortgage debt (but excluding corporate debt), surged to a record $1.2 trillion. Home mortgage debt has reached $800 billion, having increased more than $100 billion in 1978 alone. These sums are so staggering to the imagination that they are truly beyond belief. Who can possibly comprehend how much even $1 billion is, let alone $1 trillion. One billion dollars is one thousand million dollars. Think of it as a series of dollar bills stretched from end to end from here to the moon and back!

Because of sheer enormity, the size of some of the figures in this book will be difficult to grasp. They need to be presented, however, to give a sense of the scope of our problem. I fear that out of laziness or complacency, too many Americans simply don't want to be confused by the facts. Too many Americans are reluctant to face up to economic realities. Their E.Q. (economics quotient) is abysmally low. In addition, given the gigantic growth of our economy and the way statistics have been distorted by inflation, we need to be sure that we are not simply citing absolute numbers, but are showing the percentage or rate of growth in the credit and debit picture.

ITEM: In 1951, installment credit (excluding home mortgages) as a ratio of disposable income was 10. By the second quarter of 1978, it had risen to a record 19.

ITEM: In 1969, 16% of personal disposable income went to pay for housing costs. In 1979, 36% of personal disposable income went to pay housing costs.

ITEM: Federal Reserve Board figures show that the total consumer debt—including home mortgages—amounted to 25% of disposable income in 1965, and it reached a record 69% in 1978.

ITEM: Whereas credit expansion in the recession of 1974 was largely powered by business demands to augment inventories in the light of perceived shortages, in 1978–79, both the overriding demand for credit and its consequent creation originated in the consumer sector. To an ever greater degree, the burgeoning expansion of debt is being used to finance consumer consumption.

All of the above items indicate that it is not simply that the aggregate numbers have mushroomed, but that the *rate* of credit expansion has accelerated to unprecedented levels. Increased availability of easy credit comes not only through installment payment plans, credit unions, thrift institutions, and finance companies, but also through the ubiquitous plastic credit cards such as Visa, Mastercard, American Express, Carte Blanche, and Diner's Club. Credit cards have become the new key to the conduct of consumer financial affairs, and only recently have the first steps been taken to try to limit the abuses in this area.

We have become a nation of addicts to plastic fantastic money—to judge from the 600-million-plus credit cards currently in circulation. That's about 4.2 cards for each adult in the land. It is almost an absurdity to think that in a nation of 220 million Americans (including ineligible children and minors), there are more credit cards than spenders—nearly three times as many credit cards as there are people!

The creditholic has hocked 25 to 35% of his or her income for consumer goods alone, excluding home mortgages. This is an all-time record debt load. Consumer debt was nine times higher in 1979 than in 1950. Credit caters to the "we-want-it-all-now" mentality. With credit card in hand, the consumer has an easy borrowing tool without having to face the trauma or the fear of rejection of walking into a bank to fill out loan application forms. What starts out as a convenience turns into a compulsion.

The road to creditholism is smooth and well paved, and siren-song voices beckon with alluring invitations. It begins with a credit card or two. Then a few installment charge accounts are opened, and more credit cards are acquired. Then come credit unions, finance companies, an automobile loan, financing for home improvements, a vacation trip, *ad infinitum.* It seemed so painless and easy—until the bills start rolling in and the delivery of each day's mail is a dreaded event.

A segment of Walter Cronkite's evening news program featured a 35-year-old Santa Clara, California, pharmacist whose "wallet" contained 927 credit cards. This apostle of plastic fantastic power unfolded his accordian-like "billfold" to its extended length of 250 feel. It reached from his living room, beyond the long grass lawn, and ended at the sidewalk. He proudly claimed to have within his grasp the power to spend $1.25 million—all on credit. In a sense, the ability to borrow has become the measure of a person's status and presumed wealth.

Most credit-card holders are not out to make the Guinness record book, however; but many middle class consumers carry six or eight of these shiny symbols of instant cash in their wallets or purses without stretching the imagination. I personally have lost count of the number of oil company credit cards I have received in the mail and shorn with handy scissors. In a single week, three invitations to accept Visa cards were sent to me in California from New York City banks, which were engaged in a nationwide, competitive marketing program.

Now that "plastic awareness" is firmly entrenched in the United States, the marketing battle rages in Europe, which is being invaded by the new "American challenge" of U.S. credit cards. One German banker describes the sales blitz as a "credit card war with advertisements at movie theaters, cards dropping out of magazines, and application blanks lying in hotel rooms." Travelers to Finland or Yugoslavia may flash their Visa cards, which are now useable in more than 130 countries.

Not to be left out of the global reach of American credit cards, the People's Republic of China has given the green light for Visa's entry into the potentially vast China market! Can Mastercard, American Express, and Sears be far behind? In mid-1979, Visa cardholders numbered 78.1 million with an annual dollar volume of $8.9 billion, an increase of 17.5% in card holders and 30% in dollar volume from the previous year. Lagging slightly behind at 70 million card carriers was Mastercard (Master Charge), another giant in the field. Among the many other credit card issuers is Sears, which in 1979 had more than 30 million card holders.

The instant cash readily available from the widespread use of credit cards has prompted U.S. Comptroller of the Currency John Heimann to issue a stern warning. In a letter sent to 4,700 nationally chartered banks, Heimann cautioned against trying to increase a market share of consumer loans through overly aggressive promotion tactics. He expressed concern about the excessive use of credit at a time when soaring inflation and a weakening economy are making consumers vulnerable.

Time will tell whether anyone is listening to these warnings. Meanwhile, the American public's fascination with plastic power continues. Credit cards have come to be magic symbols of potency which provide instant gratification for cash-short consumers.

I am not condemning credit cards *per se.* Eight of the plastic creatures are lodged in my own wallet. I am one of those rare credit card holders (perhaps one out of ten) who assiduously avoids the 12% to 18% finance charge (depending on state laws) by paying off the full amount on or before due date. I am condemning, not the prudent use of the plastic chargers, but the accumulation of debt by an overindulgent addiction to buying now and being sorry later. Along with power goes responsibility. Those who irresponsibly abuse plastic power will discover that a downturn in the economy could make their entire house of credit cards vulnerable to collapse.

Those who cannot restrain themselves and become hungover on credit card purchases are the creditholics. Unfortunately, their collective binge spells trouble for the soundness of the economy. If they cannot resist another charge, they should either intentionally leave their cards at home or go through a withdrawal process by using their scissors to cut up one card per month, and eventually go the way of all cash.

It is no exaggeration to suggest that the use of credit cards has changed American spending habits. They are viewed as an unsecured line of credit, rather than something to be used on an emergency basis. A recent study of ten medium-sized department stores revealed that the average cash sale was $8.25, the average store–credit card sale was $15.93, and the average bank–credit card sale was $20.47. Those who dine out, according to an American Express Company report, spend up to 51% more when charging meals than when paying for them in cash.

In our present-day cultural climate, consumption is highly prized and buying is induced by blatant and by more subtle, subliminal uses of the mass media. Where wants become needs, and yesterday's luxurious frills are today's necessities, it is understandable why some 15 million Americans are in serious difficulty with overextended credit.

The American way of debt, which a later chapter will probe, has led 224,354 financially disabled persons down the path of bankruptcy in a single recent year. This amounts to more than 600 families a day! (By the summer of 1980 this figure had risen to 1,000 families per day.) Such gross figures become bloodless abstractions and don't begin to reveal the human dramas or tell the tragic tales involved. We do well to recall Bishop Gore's definition of love as "statistics with compassion." We are familiar with the "Perils of Pauline." Now come the "Perils of Plastic," as credit card delinquency rates soar. Consider the following item reported in the July 3, 1979, *Wall Street Journal.*

ITEM: With a combined income of $18,000 and a spotless credit rating, Mr. and Mrs. John D. were valued customers of the Midwestern Bank. So when the couple used up the credit line on their Visa card, the bank was more than willing to raise their borrowing limit. But after running up a $2,000 bill on the card, the couple shocked the bank by filing for personal bankruptcy. Even more of a surprise were the disclosures in the bankruptcy petition that the couple had been using 17 other credit cards from banks, oil companies, and department stores. The total tab: $32,000.[1]

Mr. and Mrs. John D. had built a house of plastic cards, and it all came tumbling down. Bankers are keeping an increasingly wary eye on the rise of credit card deadbeats. Many creditholics use one credit card to pay off the minimum charges (usually 5%) of another credit card, thereby rolling over their debts month after month and keeping the creditors at bay.

At the end of 1978, estimates were that more than $810 million Visa and Mastercard loans were in arrears—having payments 30 days or more past due. That was up 75% from about $460 million a year earlier. Crocker National Bank in San Francisco noted that its write-offs of delinquent accounts rose from $4.3 million in 1978 to approximately $6 million in 1979. Also, the publisher of the Nilson Report, a credit card newsletter, warns, "Never before in the history of our time have there been so many credit cards, so many lines of credit that exceed people's ability to repay."

Bankers realize that they are at least partially responsible for the rising credit card delinquency rates. With their aggressive national promotion campaigns and mailings, banks flooded consumers with plastic power and lowered credit standards in a frantic effort to increase their share of the market. Out of a curious mixture of guilt and self-interest, banks now encourage creditholics to seek help. To fill this need, the nonprofit Consumer Credit Counselling Service emerged and now has a national network of more than 400 branches, which serve more than 300,000 people annually. The Seattle office, for example, served more than 3,000 debt-ridden clients who needed salvaging in 1978. Incidentally, the director of the Seattle branch does not take a sanguine view of the creditholics he sees, fearing that the day is not far distant when food and fuel bills will go unmet. Credit counselors appear to be a needed and growing profession in our credit-crazed economy.

Credit cards may give a heady sense of power but one can quickly fall behind in payments and be on the credit skids. Instead of the old adage "Never a debtor be," the fervent prayer now is "Forgive us our debts." Today's conventional wisdom is to borrow and buy as much as you can get away with. "Buy now, pay later," is the way to satisfy immediate wants. Why defer gratification when you can have it all now—on credit? Payments may be deferred, but not pleasures. Some of our buying binges are irrational indeed, as in the case of the wife who grabs her credit cards and indulges in a shopping orgy every time she has a serious spat with her spouse. Can you imagine the prospects of reconciliation when the bills fall due?

Wisely used, debt can be a beneficial leverage in times of inflation, but a heavy burden in a time of deflation. It used to be considered imprudent, if not immoral, to borrow, and wise to save money. America has traditionally prided itself on being a "democracy of savers." Millions of families saved money for future needs and for the proverbial "rainy day." After all, thrift was part of the cherished legacy of the Protestant-Puritan ethic. The slogan, "It pays to save," once made eminent sense. Today it seems quaint, despite the fact that rainy days still come.

Years of chronic inflation have made savers cynical. They see prices rise like an unstoppable incoming tide, while their savings accounts silently dwindle through the erosion of the inflationary process. Not only is the purchasing power of the principal dropping, but the average savings accounts yield a mere $5\frac{1}{4}\%$ or $5\frac{1}{2}\%$, which is subject to taxes and is less than one-half of the rate of inflation. Small wonder that savers feel cheated when confronted with such a no-win situation.

Consequently, America has become a nation of spenders instead of savers. We are saving less now than at any time during the past three decades. In 1973, the rate of savings was

7.8% of disposable income. This figure dropped to 3.3% in 1979 —a meager sum when contrasted to a savings rate of 24.9% in Japan, 17.3% in France, and 15.2% in West Germany. The United States now has the lowest rate of personal savings among the industrial nations, and the rate continues to drop. These facts reflect a dramatic shift from the ethic of saving and thrift to an ethos of spending. Inflation rewards the borrower, who hopes to repay debts with cheaper dollars. Spending is encouraged, and saving seems futile.

ITEM: Bob and Judy have been married for seven years. Both are employed, and for the past five years, they saved much of Judy's earnings in a 5% savings account at the local bank. Suddenly they realized that earnings from their joint savings account of $20,000 were not keeping pace with inflation. They closed their account and used the funds for a down payment on a $97,000 home, since their friends had advised them that real estate was the best hedge against inflation. Shortly thereafter, Judy became pregnant and lost her job as a recreation director. The savings are now gone, but the mortgage payments remain. Household furnishings, a freezer, and a new washer and dryer were purchased on credit cards. Now instead of having a comfortable cushion to fall back on, they are getting deeper into debt, as they contemplate additional borrowing for a summer vacation to Canada.

Those who borrow recklessly in anticipation of being bailed out by inflation may find themselves hopelessly trapped during the down cycle of the economy. As in the old pyramid sales scheme, if you get in early and get out before the bubble bursts, you can escape unscathed. Many will be less fortunate and left holding the bag.

Consider all those families now dependent upon multiple incomes to support their style of spending. Recall that 60% of the married women in America are now in the job market. Ample credit has been extended on the basis of total household income. If one person should become ill or be laid off during a recession, and large home mortgages or equity loans must be

met, that family may find itself skating dangerously on financially thin ice.

A credit binge will surely be followed by a credit crunch.
The day of reckoning is inevitable; it can only be deferred or
postponed. If it is delayed by re-inflation—by more fiat, printing
press, paper money being issued and circulated—then the likelihood of a more resounding collapse is increased.

Paying off indebtedness, however painful, bears some resemblance to the smaller tremors associated with the California
earthquake country. If an extended period of years transpires
without news of an earthquake along the San Andreas Fault,
that becomes cause for concern. The little tremors have a way
of relieving the tension that is building up, thereby averting the
big disaster. If financial readjustments are made periodically to
relieve our credit and debit predicament, that will ease the
pressure and avert the big blow up. In this area, alas, the fault
lies not under the ground or even in the stars, but in ourselves.

For in the final analysis, the credit binge is a crisis of character. The loss of discipline and common sense breeds spending
sprees, which bring higher prices and a surge in the amount of
money needed for purchases, followed by pressure for higher
wages. This vicious upward spiral eventually leads to a point
where people lose confidence in the future value of their
money. Ultimately, the breach of confidence precipitates a collapse in the monetary system. Collapse, ironically, is the price
that is paid when the abundant life proclaimed by the Gospel
is confused with lust for material things.

Debt and credit, then, fuel inflation, which, in turn, stimulates more indebtedness. The critical problem with inflation is
its aftermath. Many people may ride its roller-coaster to dizzying heights of prosperity. But there are limits. The roller-
coaster that goes up also lurches downward and will catch many
unprepared and breathless during its harrowing downward descent.

Those who sow the wind are destined to reap the whirlwind.
Those who borrow money heavily in hopes of being rescued by
inflation may be living on borrowed time as well. For Ameri-

cans to be encumbered with excessive credit card consumer debts is to sell our birthright of freedom and independence for a mess of pottage.

Reckless spenders, overextended debtors, extravagent high-livers, real-estate speculators, as well as highly leveraged corporations can find themselves caught in a liquidity squeeze and discover that they simply cannot borrow additional funds to meet their immediate obligations. Their options are to re-trench, sell their assets at a loss, and change their life styles, or to default and declare bankruptcy. The latter option will be explored in the chapter on bankruptcy. Forced liquidation of debt is not a pleasant prospect. Sacrifice, financial disorder, agony, pain, dashed dreams, community stigma, the sense of failure and futility, unpaid mortgages, unemployment, misery could become the unwelcomed scenario for millions when plastic power turns into plastic perils.

The erosion of public confidence plus overextension of debt and credit, added to the high rates of inflation, low levels of saving, and the decline in productivity comprise a dangerous and potentially explosive mix for the American economy. If and when the economic collapse does come, the fall will be hard for the overextended creditholics who lack an adequate financial cushion.

Our discussion in this opening chapter has set forth the ingredients for a deepening loss of confidence, which could precipitate a credit crash. An apt metaphor of our economic prospect is that we are riding in an upward-bound elevator on a sinking ship. Though it seems as if progress is being made, in reality the entire ship is taking on water and is in danger of going to the bottom.

What our response might be as Christians will be reviewed in the final chapter. Suffice it to say here that in our dismay with a world out of balance, Christians have a special mandate, which compels them to care and to share. We have not only a garden, but also the obligation to share its fruits with one another. Indeed, the biblical theme of deliverance from captivity is a challenge for countless middle-class Americans—who have

mortgaged their futures by incurring an abundance of debt—
to seek liberation from their bondage to material possessions.

Consumerism is the prepackaged life style that is retailed in
our culture. Whenever we consider buying into its value premises, we would do well to raise alternative Christian questions
about appropriate choices and priorities concerning the purpose of life and the primacy of faith. What are the claims of the
Gospel upon those who are addicted to lives of comfort and ease
amidst a suffering world? Biblical faith is a summons to repentance. In our debt-ridden context, repentance means a change
in life style, a turning away from self-serving profligacy to care,
commitment, and concern for neighbor. These issues will receive fuller attention later on in this volume. Meanwhile, we
turn our focus in the next chapter to a clearer understanding
of the role of the banking system in fueling the flames of debt
and credit.

II

Fuel for the Fire:
The Banking System

Banks contribute to inflation by expanding credit. In fact, banks are credit-creating machines. An individual deposits money in the bank. Those funds do not stay put, but are put to use. In a sense, they are not really deposits, that is, funds placed in the bank's vaults for safekeeping until the depositor calls for them.

The word "deposit" conjures up visions of piles of coins and stacks of paper bills. Actually deposits are the sum total of money *promised* by the bank to those who entrust it with their funds. Deposits are money which depositors, in effect, lend to the bank on a short-term basis, repayable on demand. The bank, in turn, loans this money out to borrowers on a longer term basis, thereby extending credit. The borrower in this case has increased purchasing power, which is not offset by an equal decrease in the purchasing power of the saver.

To illustrate this bewildering process, let us take an example. If you, ("A") deposit $1,000 at your friendly neighborhood bank, the bank will turn around and lend $850, or 85%, of that $1,000 to a borrower ("B"). That $1,000 of yours has now grown to $1,850, on paper at least. Borrower "B" may draw checks against his or her $850. These checks are deposited either in the same bank or in other banks, and 85% of these deposited funds may be loaned out to "C." The loans of one bank increase the deposits of another bank. This process continues so long as each bank maintains the legal reserve requirement of 15%. It is known as the "fractional reserve banking system," which was begun in 1913 with the establishment of the Federal Reserve System.

As baffling as it may sound, we may say that modern banks do not lend money. What the banker lends is the bank's credit —in which the borrower has confidence. To return to our example, your original $1,000 has grown to $2,572.50. And so the credit expansion continues by the miracle of the multiplier effect that is ingeniously employed by the banking system. Bank deposits and bank loans have a way of blowing bigger the bubble of debt.

In the discussion that follows, I have no deliberate intention of denigrating bankers or demeaning the venerable institution of banking. Some of my good friends are bankers. Everyone knows that bankers are held in lofty esteem and occupy a position of impeccable community respect—having recovered from their fall from grace during the Great Depression era and immediately thereafter. At least in recent decades, a banker's name has become synonymous with probity and is certainly less questionable than the images associated with Wall Street or Madison Avenue.

In passing, however, we might note that, historically, moneylenders and money changing have not always enjoyed such favor or respect. Prior to the rise of modern industrial capitalism, bankers were more likely to be viewed as villains rather than as heroes. They were frequently caricatured as greedy, rapacious, and oppressive tyrants. If not the oldest profession in the world, surely the professional moneylender is among its early ones. In ancient Greece, Demosthenes (384–322 B.C.) was recorded as having employed his extraordinary rhetorical skills to defend Phormio, a moneylender, from the prejudices and hostilities of an Athenian jury.

That great soldier-statesman of ancient Rome, Marcus Porcius Cato (234–149 B.C.), once remarked that lending money at interest was not honorable and was akin to murder and pimping. Then we have Dante, one of the greatest poets of the Middle Ages, painting an absolutely horrifying picture of the moneylender in his classic "Inferno" section of the *Divine Comedy.* Inferno is Dante's Hell, where he consigns the worst sinners who suffer there an unending and terrible agony. In the outermost rim of the seventh circle, where the sand was furnace-hot and "with a slow fall, fire was raining in dilated flakes" —there sits our villain, the moneylender, grief gushing from his eyes.

Indeed, the banking profession has come a long way from the depths of the Inferno to the pedestal of paradise. Since banking is so highly regarded nowadays, it may come as a surprise to learn that the institution of moneylending with interest was disapproved of by Aristotle and Cicero and the early church fathers. Until the reign of Henry VIII in England, interest-taking was forbidden by both the canon and the civil law, and violators of these strictures were subject to severe penalty.

I cite these instances of historical antipathy toward the merchants of debt not as an idle diversion, but to point out that even today one finds ambivalence toward bankers. These mixed feelings are subconscious and deep-seated emotions of love-hate or honor-contempt between borrowers and lenders. There is gratitude for the loan but contempt for the creditor. The moneylender is gladly sought but bitterly hated. When the masks are stripped away, the ambivalence will surface.

During the days of student revolution in Berkeley and other campus communities in the sixties, banks were a favorite target of student stridency. Time and time again, bricks and rocks were thrown at bank windows. Shattered glass littered the sidewalks. It was a familiar sight to see glass company trucks parked in front of banks while repairs were being made. Finally, the banks must have grown impatient with all the stones being thrown at glass houses; they removed the window panes and substituted brick walls. They began to look more like mighty fortresses than modern bank buildings. The sixties was one of those periods when the shadow side of the ambivalence of feelings toward banks surfaced among the student generation of protestors.

With the return of quiescence on the campus in the seventies, student hostility toward banks subsided. The glass exterior has returned—presumably to convey that more inviting, intimate feeling of openness and to discourage robberies by increased public visibility.

As a matter of fact, however, bank robberies have increased dramatically. If the younger generation found banks to be a favorite target in the sixties, the criminal element has virtually declared open season on banks since the late seventies. A new record was set in New York City when 120 bank robberies were committed during the first 21 days of August in 1979. Of course, Los Angeles was not going to be outstripped by New York. L.A. can claim 127 heists in a single month during the same summer. Meanwhile, back in "Fun City," there were ten bank robberies, plus the plucking clean of $2 million cash from a Brink's armored car parked in front of Chase Manhattan Bank's main headquarters in the financial district, on one day. Actually, the record had been set one month earlier when 13 robberies occurred in one day. In the first eight months of 1979, more than 606 bank robberies were committed in New York City—a 30% increase from the previous year.

I am not sure what this rash of robberies means. One city official blames it on inflation—presumably the high cost of living for criminals! Although this explanation sounds silly at first, criminologist Robert Blakey of Cornell University seriously suggests that the high rate of heists could be due to an economic downturn.

In view of present-day sophisticated alarms, video equipment, and surveillance techniques employed by most banks, the burgeoning bank robberies are an enigma. Either criminals are becoming more desperate these days or else banks are an easy mark, regardless of their architectural style. In any case, the ambivalent love-hate relationship persists toward banks—even among criminals.

Normally, the attitudes of confidence and trust in bankers and the banking system prevails over the feelings of doubt. However, a cursory glance at the history of moneylending—where originally usury meant any profit, however large or small, taken for the loan of money—should not make us overly sanguine about the institution of moneylending.

Public confidence in the banks is absolutely essential for the banking system to remain viable. Banks borrow for the short term and loan their funds on a longer term basis. Only about 5% of deposits are on hand as cash. The remainder is loaned out or invested. It would not take much—perhaps only 5% of the depositors demanding their funds on a given day—for a bank to feel the drain. Confidence is the steadying, invisible hand that sustains the banking system. If people's confidence should buckle, if they should run out of confidence, they will surely run to their banks. If confidence should waver, then the chilling dictum that Paul Erdman gives his audiences rings true: "Today we wait in gas lines; tomorrow we will wait in bank lines."

Some students of banking practices would argue that the policy of borrowing short and lending on a longer term basis has led to panic and depression in the past. Robert de Fremery contends that a confidence crisis is inevitable under the banking system of borrowing short and lending long. Such practice, which de Fremery dubs "BSALL," is unsound and creates instability. It results in a multiplication of deposits that exist only as book entries. It literally permits banks not only to lend funds but also to create money out of nonexistent dollars, thus rendering the monetary system vulnerable. As de Fremery notes, "Banks cannot promise to pay out a larger and larger number of non-existent dollars without causing a loss of confidence."[4] He explains that no individual in his or her right mind would borrow $1,000 with a due date of one month and then turn around and loan that $1,000 to someone else for six months. If an individual were to ask a banker if it is prudent to borrow short and lend long, that banker would call the person a fool. And yet, charges de Fremery, banks engage in such foolishness with abandon.

In the past when confidence has been shattered, we have witnessed the bank panics of 1873, 1884, 1893, and 1907. Even though the Federal Reserve System was established on December 23, 1913, to prevent runs on banks and to provide an "elastic currency as a lender of last resort," the Fed failed to stem the tide of bank failures during the Depression. After many of the states had already declared bank moratoria, President Franklin D. Roosevelt finally ordered a national "bank holiday" in March, 1933.

The deepening depression in business in the years 1930, 1931, and 1932 led to failures among some of the larger city banks. Already there had been a high mortality rate among smaller country banks serving in agricultural areas. In December, 1930, the Bank of the United States, located in New York City, was the first large urban bank to close its doors. With its rather presumptuous and highly visible name, the failure of this particular bank sent out a shock wave with its rippling effect that was deeply disturbing to other already nervous large city banks. Those who adhere to the conviction that real estate values are a "sure bet" which can only go up will be sobered by the realization that when the Bank of the United States faltered it was heavily involved in mortgage loans based on real estate values in New York City.

Annual reports from the Federal Reserve Board show that in 1930, 1,345 banks suspended payments to depositors. In 1931, bank suspensions hit a record high of 2,298, with aggregate deposits at $1,691,510,000. In 1932, the number of suspensions was 1,456, with deposits totaling $715,626,000. In 1933, 408 banks had closed their doors by March when President Roosevelt intervened to declare the bank holiday. During the six-year period between 1929 and 1936, a total of 8,559 banks suspended operations tying up $6,400,000,000. In fairness, it must be pointed out that this record covers the worst economic period in our history. These figures should not obscure the fact that many thousands of billions of dollars have been exchanged without failure or default by banks. Historians generally agree, however, that the first wave of bank failures in 1930–1931 played a crucial role in converting a serious recession into a deep depression.

Incidentally, across the seas Europe was equally caught up in a bank panic. The ripple was created when the Credit Anstalt in Austria collapsed in May, 1931. A month later, all the German banks were closed as the alarm spread throughout the country.

One way the U.S. government has sought to engender confidence is with the guarantee that depositors are insured for up to $100,000 (up recently from $40,000) by the Federal Deposit Insurance Corporation (FDIC). According to a published report from the FDIC, the amount of depositors' funds under coverage amounted to $693 billion at the end of 1977. Yet the total reserve in the FDIC insurance fund is only $7.2 billion, with a statutory provision to borrow an additional $3 billion in case of an emergency. Note that if only 1% of the nation's deposits were to be wiped out through bank failures, the entire FDIC fund would be exhausted.

Twenty years earlier, in the 1957 FDIC annual report was the statement: "There is no question that the present deposit insurance would be entirely inadequate if, for example, a situation such as that of 1930–1933 should recur." In 1957, there was $1.46 in the FDIC funds behind every $100.00 of insured deposits; whereas, in 1977, only $1.15 stood behind every $100.00. Moreover, the amount of uninsured funds has ballooned from $98.5 billion in 1957 to $307 billion in 1977, due to the growth of the banking system and the number of large depositors beyond the $40,000 range under coverage. This sum of $307 billion *not* under FDIC insurance is significant. As the American Bankers Association has warned: "The realization on the part of large depositors that their deposits are not fully covered might cause them in a time of uncertainty to shift some of their deposits." Such a shift could precipitate an erosion of confidence and set off a chain reaction.

In 1975, when the Franklin National Bank failed, $3.54 billion were necessary to effect a rescue mission. Franklin was only a $5-billion bank in the first place. Imagine the prospects if one or two of the nation's large banks should sink. Those meager FDIC funds would be depleted in short order. Most bankers, when queried about such matters, merely shrug their shoulders and reply that the government would simply print more money to bail them out. This is surely a show of confidence. Recall that following the crash of 1929, President Herbert Hoover twice reassured the American people that the Federal Reserve System had made our banks panic proof. Yet the Federal Reserve Board's annual reports note that 5,099 banks suspended payment during the next three years.

My purpose in recounting these details is not to be a panic-monger, but simply to show that without confidence the people perish. If confidence should sag, a general run on the banks is plausible. In the initial phase of an erosion of confidence in banks, depositors will start withdrawing their funds. Bankers will pull back on loans. This act of curtailing loans intensifies the loss of public confidence. If a banker should continue to create more loans while there is a drain on deposits, however, he places himself in a worse position. In either case, once confidence is impaired, banks are in a bind.

The Federal Reserve System, the nation's central bank and lender of last resort, requires member banks to maintain on deposit with it an equivalent per cent of their deposit liabilities. The current requirement is 7% of demand deposits up to $2 million and up to 16¼% of deposits in excess of $400 million and 3% of savings deposits. No interest is paid to the banks on these reserves. Given today's high interest rates, plus the limitations imposed upon these funds which the banks might otherwise use for profit-making ventures, many banks are withdrawing from the Federal Reserve System. In 1947, about half of all banks were members of the Fed. They accounted for 85% of all bank deposits. In the past decade, 600 banks have left the Fed. Those still in the system now account for 40% of all banks and 72% of total deposits.

The trend toward withdrawal from the Fed has increasingly been a concern to banking and government officials. It means less control by the Fed over the banking system. Fed spokesmen have cautiously warned that as deposits used for settlement purposes are increasingly held outside the Federal Reserve, the banking system becomes more exposed to the risk that such funds might be immobilized if a large correspondent bank outside the Federal Reserve should experience substantial operating difficulties or liquidity problems.

Moreover, there is the problem of thinning capital reserves as banks withdraw from the Federal Reserve System to escape the reserve requirement. Sufficient reserves are necessary to meet losses from bad loans, delinquent payments, and declines in the market value of securities or bonds held in bank investment portfolios.

Chairman Irving H. Sprague of the FDIC noted that ten years ago there were no banks with more than $1 billion in deposits in trouble and only two with more than $100 million in deposits on the trouble list. As of April 30, 1979, Sprague reported that five banks in the $1 billion-plus category of deposits were in trouble, and 30 banks with deposits of $100 million to $1 billion were on the list. As of April 30, 1979, there were 317 "problem banks" reported in all.

During the recession of 1974, the leading business journals were buzzing with news about the potential hazards of vulnerable banks; in fact, bank analysts were "making a list" of banks in jeopardy and noting their questionable loans to the REITS (real estate investment trusts); loans for global tankers (which were in oversupply); heavy commitments with New York City municipal bonds (on the brink of default); loans outstanding to Penn Central and Lockheed, and foreign loans to developing nations or to dictatorships that were in danger of being toppled.

The overextension of credit by the banks was troubling the regulators, government officials, and many banking authorities.

"There is concern about American banks' exposure everywhere, particularly in developing countries. Everyone is talking about possible defaults," said Fred H. Klopstock, an advisor with the Federal Reserve Bank of New York.[5]

During 1975, the nation's banks wrote off $3 billion in bad loans, the highest amount in banking history. A group of seven New York City banks accounted for approximately 40% of the total. First National City Bank and Chase Manhattan Bank took the largest write-offs, primarily from the inability of borrowers to pay off debts due on real estate and corporate loans.

For example, the bankruptcy of the retail giant W. T. Grant caught banks holding $640 million in Grant paper. These charge-offs did not reflect the reduced market value of loans to municipal borrowers or the doubtful loans abroad to nations mired in financial or political turmoil and considered to be "uncreditworthy." The fact that major banks continued to loan funds to these high-risk nations appears to confirm the suspicion that banks poured in money simply to stretch out and keep their debtors afloat, since write-offs would have had a dramatic impact in shaking the public's confidence in the banks.

Senator Frank Church has expressed the concern that Congress could one day find itself forced to vote aid to debtor nations that are in danger of defaulting on their loans simply to preserve the stability of the U.S. banking system. The international banking field is traditionally a secretive, hush-hush operation. Whether full disclosure is a bane or a blessing, so far as engendering public confidence is concerned, remains a moot question.

Still another source of vulnerability for banks is the sizeable amounts of funds OPEC nations have deposited with large New York banks on a short-term basis. Information on these matters is highly guarded, but the best estimates are that Saudi Arabia alone has $40 billion in short-term funds, principally certificates of deposit (C.D.'s) concentrated in large U.S. banks. If such funds were to be withdrawn abruptly, it could create dislocations, at least temporarily, or even send shock waves through the banking system.

The recession of 1974 tested the resiliency of the banks. Fortunately public confidence did not buckle. Even one of the stronger banks, not linked with the troubles of New York City, the Bank of America, had 10% of its total equity tied up in a computer firm that was on the brink of bankruptcy. In a serious recession, a rash of corporate bankruptcies could precipitate a breach of confidence among bank depositors.

Recall that during New York City's financial fiasco there was considerable snickering across the nation. Small-town folks in remote places chortled and gleefully felt it was high time for the "Big Apple" to get its comeuppance, for it served those city slickers right. Anti-urban animosity—a latent condition of small-town America—surfaced in full force. Sympathy for the plight of "Fun City" was in short supply, until the realization dawned that if New York City—the country's financial capital, if not the world's—were to "go down the tube," the city's major banks would be in jeopardy, because they were large holders of its municipal bonds. If these big banks were to go under, the whole nation would be implicated in a financial panic the likes of which would probably make the 1930s look like a picnic. And so, at the end of the day, the nation heaved a huge sigh of relief when the Congress voted to guarantee some $1.6 billion worth of New York City paper. The crisis was averted or perhaps postponed to await another dramatic round. Some wags say the crisis was merely papered over—thanks to Uncle Sam in whom the people trust. Once again, public confidence was restored, at least temporarily.

How vulnerable New York City remains and how many other municipalities are in such dire financial binds (such as Cleveland, Detroit, Toledo, Newark) that they will need to be rescued from the brink of bankruptcy is still an open question. This much is clear: If confidence should waver and faith be suspended, the financial structure that is supported by the banks and the federal government will once again be tested and tried.

Banks continue to add fuel to the fire of debt and credit expansion. They are the chief marketers of Visa and Mastercard credit cards, which facilitate consumer borrowing and spending. They play a key role in mortgage lending for real estate purchase or refinancing.

Financial analysts have noted that economic recovery from the 1974–1975 recession has been carried largely on the shoulders of consumers. A good share of the funds for the consumer spending spree has come from the direct-mail inducements of banks offering home owners "equity loans" on the inflated values of their property. Some of these funds are also used to speculate on purchases of additional real estate.

Note that a modest home purchased for $100,000—not an unusual price these days—might carry a 30-year mortgage for $80,000.[6] At the going 13% mortgage rate, this amounts to an $896.00 monthly payment for the first mortgage alone. Add to this, $1,500 a year for taxes and $35.00 a month for insurance. Such payments call for families who either have substantial earnings or are committed to high levels of borrowing. Their burdens could turn out to be crushing during any period of economic adversity.

Talk to finance company officers or bankers about the debt load consumers are carrying, and they generally respond that the public is better able to handle debts nowadays, when the rate of inflation is soaring. They do not seem overly concerned about the burden of borrowing or the debt traps that many illiquid consumers have fallen into. After all, their business is to make loans, to extend credit. And it is a highly competitive business. In some respects, to ask moneylenders about the status of debt is like asking General Patton if he likes to engage in battle.

An entirely different picture emerges, however, when one talks to consumer credit counselors, who seek to bind the wounds of the casualties and victims of overborrowing. Counselors located in every geographical section of the nation are plainly worried about their clients who are drowning in a sea of debt. The picture is complicated today by the fact that many households are living fully up to, and even beyond, the totality of two incomes. If the economy should falter, or take even a modest downturn, the concern is that bills for such basic necessities as food, utilities, and heating will go unmet.

The policies and practices of both the banks and the federal government add fuel to the fire, since they are prime generators in credit and debt expansion. They seem oblivious to the fact that funneling massive amounts of money into our already inflated economy is like an alcoholic on a binge taking yet another drink, or like staving off pneumonia by incurring a constant fever, and hoping that the fever can be contained at levels that will not kill the patient.

The next chapter reviews in detail the role of the federal government in adding to the debt pyramid.

III

The Debt Pyramid: Role of the Federal Government

Excessive debt and credit at all levels of spending is the Achilles' heel through which public confidence has been eroded and the stubborn rate of inflation has remained unchecked. In an uncharacteristically perplexed mood, one of Wall Street's most respected analysts has been imploring the Universe to send a New Messiah to deliver us from our state of economic confusion. While one may rejoice in the salubrity of Wall Street seeking transcendent redress, the particular shape or voice such a New Messiah might assume surely makes for conjecture.

Quite possibly, the new bearer of "Glad Tidings" would confront the federal government in much the same manner as the prophet Nathan confronted the unsuspecting King David for his indiscretions. When the king said, "The man who has done this deserves to die," the prophet quickly replied: "You are the man." (2 Sam. 12:5, 7)

When it comes to a discussion of debt and credit, there is no more critical place on which to focus attention than the federal government—possessor of the only legitimate monopoly to print money on its own printing press. Our nation today faces the most massive long-term fixed debt and credit structure in the entire history of the human race. The figures are so massive that they literally boggle the brain.

ITEM: If the public debts for national, state, and local governments are combined, the figure amounts to more than $1 trillion—or $4,811 for every man, woman, and child. Note that this sum is not to be confused with private consumer debts previously reviewed. If the public debt is added to all other forms of private and corporate debt, the figure rises astoundingly to $3.36 trillion—or $16,000 per person. I am told that $3,360,000,000,000 is a conservative estimate. The sum could well be over $5 trillion!

ITEM: It took the national debt 27 years to double—from $200 to $400 billion by 1971. Then it took less than 8 years to double again, when it pierced through the $800 billion ceiling level on April 9, 1979. At the time of the passing of the Federal Reserve Act on December 23, 1913, the national debt was a mere $1.3 billion.

With figures like the above, it is not altogether facetious to suggest that the Office of the Secretary of the Treasury should be redesignated "Secretary of Debt." Seemingly the national debt knows no limits. In September, 1979, Congress defeated a proposal to lift the debt ceiling by an additional $99 billion. Several weeks later, a compromise bill was finally approved raising the debt ceiling by $49 billion to the new height of $879 billion. The entire process is certain to be repeated. Predictably, Congress will debate and delay until the eleventh hour, holding up bond offerings and creating concern among the 30 million recipients of Social Security checks and others on the federal payroll. Much rhetoric will be heard trying to shift the blame around. However, the whole thing is a charade. For if the request is denied, the United States government will be in a state of technical default!

With the national debt approaching the $900 billion mark, we have come light years from the conviction expressed by President Van Buren in his third annual address to Congress when he urged that there can be no justification for a national debt in times of peace and that the federal government should have its finances unencumbered. Whether we conceive of our national debt accumulation as capable of infinite growth or as a bubble that will burst when its time is due, it is an enigma which cannot be relegated simply to the attic of benign neglect forever.

Debt and credit is an Achilles' heel, for it contributes more and more to volatility during inflationary booms and, conversely, will act in the same manner during deflation.

When debts are incurred by individuals, it is obvious that regular payments fall due. If these payments go unmet, in due time creditors will press their claims. With the federal government, payments also fall due. But deficits are allowed to accumulate, and the national debt continues to build up in a never-ending pyramid. It is estimated that taxpayers ante up between $60 and $75 *billion* annually just to pay interest on *our* national debt.

Few people seemed concerned about the national debt, which is no longer creeping but galloping upward with giant strides. A few years ago, America's most prominent economist, writer of a leading textbook in the field and a distinguished professor at MIT, responded to a worried reader's query about the national debt in his syndicated column. In effect, his casual reply was, "Don't worry your pretty head about it. Just let the economists deal with those issues." I could hardly believe such a cavalier response. We now know that war is too important to be left to the generals, for our fate is at stake. So, too, economics is too important to be left to the economists. As a matter of fact, their batting average in recent years has not been anything to write home about. Better to say, "I don't know," than to insult the intelligence of the American public, counsel neglect ("benign" or otherwise), or make a gnostic faith out of their dismal science.

Peter Drucker, who, of course, is no flaming conservative, believes it is now generally accepted by almost everyone—except ministers of finance—that money is far too important to be entrusted to politicians and governments. Drucker observes, "It is even increasingly accepted by ordinary people who know no economics but who see the purchasing power of their earnings decline month after month. Surely no one, perhaps not even the ministers of finance, any longer believes . . . that governments have both the competence and the integrity to manage money responsibly and non-politically."[7]

The national debt is a link to our inflationary spiral. Inflation, as every shopper knows, is increasing prices and decreasing purchasing power, more money required to buy fewer goods. Actually there are two broad categories or sources of inflation. "Price inflation" is reflected in the general price level moving up or the pattern of prices rising in nearly all things. "Monetary inflation" is when the federal government allows the existing amount of money to increase by increasing the money supply. Hence, the so-called monetarist school argues that government causes inflation by excessive creation of money supply.

Actually, Milton Friedman, guru of the monetarist school, advocates a steady, moderate increase in the money supply at a 3% to 5% annual growth rate so as to produce continuous economic growth. Note that the actual rate of monetary growth is on the order of 10% to 12% for 1978 and 1979, which is highly inflationary. Despite the Federal Reserve's repeated effort over the past five years, in the pre-Volker era, to create the impression that it has been pursuing a policy aimed at winding down inflation, its actions have actually been doing the opposite.

Friedman argues against sharp swings in monetary policy and notes that a steady course of monetary growth is associated with periods of relative economic stability; whereas wide swings in the rate of monetary growth have also been periods of wide fluctuations in economic activity.

Despite former Treasury Secretary William E. Simon's charge that "Inflation should wear a label: 'Made and Manufactured in Washington, D.C.,' " I would not want to put the entire onus of inflation solely on the government's shoulders, although it is true that government does play a major role. (Parenthetically, I cannot help wondering why Simon did not do a better job while he was riding in the saddle during the days of Nixonomics).

Inflation is not simply a problem of supply and demand. Too many distortions are at work. There are the intense pressures of labor and strong labor organizations negotiating wage settlements, which become inflationary in what is referred to as "cost-push" inflation. Moreover, large corporations, with a keen eye to profit margins, are adept at "cost-push" or pushing up prices even higher than the margins required by increased wages. Prices are often hiked prior to or in anticipation of increased costs for labor and materials or on the basis of rumors of prospective price controls.

Consumers, too, stimulate inflation by accelerated purchases, hoarding, bidding up prices by saving less and spending more, and by enlarging mortgage and installment debts, which is precisely what consumers by the droves have been doing with "equity loans" taken out on their inflated real estate property values. Consumers can set off what is known as "demand-pull" inflation or the pulling up of prices. Simply stated, one could point to wage-inflation, price-inflation, and consumer demand–inflation. We can see that Big Government, Big Corporation, Big Labor, and Big Consumer all have a hand in the inflationary process.

We are at a frustrating time when the finger of blame is being pointed in every possible direction for the spiraling rise in inflation. It seems easier to find a scapegoat than to confess to one's own responsibility. Big Labor blames Big Business. Big Business blames Big Government. Big Government blames Big OPEC. The poor blame the wealthiest Americans who comprise 7% of the families but receive more income than the entire bottom half of the nation's population. The $400 billion income of the top 7% of the population is larger than the entire federal budget. This income provides a powerful spending source of discretionary funds for fueling inflation. Meanwhile, the rich blame the poor for the burgeoning welfare costs and transfer payments. Feeling caught in the squeeze and lacking the tax benefits of the rich or the welfare privileges of the poor, the middle class is growing restless and rebellious. In this season of discontent, there is no shortage of casting blame when it comes to the vexing problem of inflation.

Milton Friedman has been helpful in pointing out that "money does matter," that the supply of money itself, which is largely dictated by policies of the federal government, can be a major source of economic dislocation. His extensive studies lead to the conclusion that every major inflation has been produced by monetary expansion—usually to meet the overriding demands of war, which have forced the creation of more money to supplement taxation. One might say that governments declare war and must eventually find a way to pay for their war games.

Two key inflation policy matters rest directly at the doorstep of the federal government: the supply of money and the amount of government spending.

The supply of money is regulated by the government. If the U.S. Treasury needs money to pay its bills, it can sell new bonds printed on attractively engraved paper to the Federal Reserve banks. The Federal Reserve pays for the bonds by increasing the Treasury's deposit account. The Treasury writes checks to pay its bills on this account. These checks are deposited in commercial banks which in turn can create credit through the fractional reserve system previously discussed. Moreover, the Federal Reserve Board can create money out of thin air by simply writing a check on itself without necessarily making a deposit to back that check. Only the Fed has this awesome prerogative—and in unlimited amounts. Through the magic identified long ago by Adam Smith as the "multiplier effect," when the Fed writes a check for $100 million, it actually sets in motion a money-creating process that ends up becoming more than $600 million as it circulates through the economy.

This complex process of money creation is clearly illustrated in the following chart prepared by *The New York Times:*

If you are ever in the mood to start an argument, bring up the subject of government spending. It is likely to raise the

How the U.S. Creates More Money

The Process of Money Creation by The Federal Reserve Board

Start

The Federal Reserve Board's open market committee instructs Alan R. Holmes of The Federal Reserve Bank of New York to purchase Government securities.

↓

Mr. Holmes writes a check to buy $100 million in Treasury Bills from Salomon Brothers

↓

Salomon Brothers has $100 million more cash, but correspondingly less in Treasury Bills

↙

Salomon Brothers deposits $100 million in Citibank.

↙

Citibank puts $15 million back in Fed as "Reserve Requirement" and loans $85 million to United States Steel.

↓

U.S. Steel has $85 million more cash but a debt to Citibank

↙

U.S. Steel deposits $85 million in The Pittsburgh National Bank.

↙

Pittsburgh National puts $13 million in its reserve account at the Fed and uses remaining $72 million to buy notes of the city of Boston.

↙

Boston has $72 million more cash, but a debt to Pittsburgh National

↑

The process continues until with a 15 percent "Reserve Requirement," Mr. Holmes' original check for $100 million adds more than $600 million to the total of bank deposits in the nation.

Finish

The Multiplier Effect

Reprinted with permission *New York Times Chart*

hackles of liberals and conservatives alike. The fact is that the nation's largest employer is now government—in its federal, state, and local forms. Government employs more workers than the automobile, steel, and all other durable-goods manufacturers *combined.* One out of every six workers in America is now on the public payroll. The federal government alone spends at the rate of $1 billion per day. With stakes that monumental, the government must be viewed as part of the inflationary problem, and not simply its cure.

The matter of government spending brings up the problem of budget deficits, whose yearly pace we have grown accustomed to. Government deficits mean that the federal government is spending more on purchases and other transfer payments than the amount of money it can pay for with tax revenues. Deficit spending is a notion introduced to American politics by Lord John Maynard Keynes, the erudite British economist and man of affairs who made a fortune in bed, speculating on the world's currency market before breakfast while others slept. Lord Keynes justified deficits during economic slack periods to "prime the pump" or stimulate the economy's recovery. His prescription may have worked when the Depression hit rock bottom; however, what worked for a Depression was not intended to be necessary during inflation. Yet federal spending continues to exceed revenues. Year after year we have seen a perennial string of deficits accumulating. In fact, the federal government has rolled up budget deficits in 20 of the past 21 years. The cumulative deficit for the years 1975–1978 is in excess of $200 billion; thus the government's fiscal policy inevitably makes a major contribution to inflationary pressures. The logical question arises: if budget deficits to the tune of $25 to $60 billion are required for the *recovery* years between 1975 and 1979, can you possibly imagine the sums that will be necessary for pump priming during the next deflationary cycle? Can we afford to let the economists worry about this alone?

Government deficits are inflationary when accompanied by an increase in money, as is usually the case. A large government debt issue usually drives interest rates upward and could not be marketed without a large increase in money supply. Government creates not only the debt, but also the money to buy it. Government deficits, therefore, increase the supply of money and also accelerate the velocity of money, since government spends its money more rapidly than individuals do.

To be sure, there are benefits to government spending. But notice the snickering and sneering that goes on among so many Americans whenever the topic is brought up for discussion.

The military establishment is a favorite whipping boy and probably for good reason. During a visit to a military base, I was personally escorted to see a "billion-dollar misunderstanding" —an underground antimissile system which became obsolete even before its completion and now sits abandoned. One wonders how many other misguided projects have been funded with the public's money.

Many Americans cannot help wincing when we read about the sizeable amount of taxpayer funds ($17 million) spent to remodel and redecorate the former homes occupied by Richard Nixon in Key Biscayne, Florida, and San Clemente, California, plus the continuing payments that are required to subsidize his retinue and his regal life style—at taxpayers' expense.

If you want to see an obscene sight, take a look at the number of limosines (with their engines and air conditioners running and chauffers waiting) lined up near the congressional office buildings for the "convenience" of our public "servants." It makes taxpayers wonder cynically if such conspicuous consumption—with *our* funds—is really necessary. And yet the public tolerates such political pornography.

The annual or biannual travel junkets to far-off, exotic places that our members of Congress take on the pretext of "investigating" are a sham and a scam on the public purse. The perks of political office are a pique to the public. Any test of performance applied to Congress would surely challenge its complacency, its tedious unresponsiveness to resolving burning national issues, its mastery of the art of self-preservation, its archaic system of committee warlordism.

Widespread suspicion abounds that the sense of "public

trust," which elected officials have sworn to uphold, has been violated. Small wonder that the taxpayers' revolt is gaining ground nationwide, that people are angry and are calling for national budget limitations upon spending—loudly, if not clearly. If elected officials shirk their responsibility, then some public control on federal pursestrings is necessary in order to realign priorities. Small wonder that public confidence in political decision-makers has waned so that their credibility has worn thin. A spendthrift government makes talk of economy empty prattle.

One has the feeling that the number and amount of government subsidies through any one of a thousand programs and agencies—not simply to the poor on welfare, but to agribusiness, ailing industries (such as Chrysler), and corporate coffers—are so vast that to open up that thorny subject to scrutiny would be to unlock a Pandora's box, doubtless the habitat for thousands of lobbyists representing special-interest groups. Raising the tax burden to pay for government spending has its limits before it backfires into political liability and electoral reprisals at the polls. One wonders, therefore, if there is substance to the suspicion that the federal government deliberately contributes to inflation as a way of bailing itself out of its own debt burdens. No less an authority than Keynes has charged that it is through the process of inflation that governments can secretly and arbitrarily confiscate an important part of the wealth of their citizens, impoverishing many but enriching some. Keynes warned specifically that debauching the currency was a sure road to destruction.

However circuitously, our discussion leads inevitably to the subject of money. I am painfully aware that many religiously oriented folks—both lay and clergy—profess public disdain or nonchalance about discussing money—while privately coveting it. Perhaps this is one reason why there is so little serious reflection on the subject. Preachers are wont to stress that we are more apt to worship at the throne of money than to use money in the service of God. Since this point is generally acknowledged, it too is a conversation stopper.

First we must acknowledge that there exists a long and controversial history about the meaning of money—what it is and what it does, how it influences human behavior for good and for ill, why it is a bane or a blessing. In a sense the whole history of civilization is the saga of money—the account of the human endeavor to create it, to earn it, to spend it, to control it, to save it, to live with it or with too little of it. It is the story of conflicts and wars over money, the role of money in the rise and fall of empires, the mismanagement, malpractice, and temptations of money. Perhaps more easily than anything else, money ignites those deep human emotions of greed and fear.

I do not intend to enter the debate about the ontology or the essence of money—whether or not it has intrinsic or extrinsic value. For our purposes we may proceed with the assumption that money is what money does.

Simply stated, money is a device to permit people to exchange goods and services and to repay their debts in a more convenient manner than by direct barter. What makes checks, paper money, and coins acceptable at face value as payments for debts? Essentially it is the confidence of people that they will be able to exchange such money for real goods and services whenever they wish to do so. The use of money is based on trust. Without an implicit vote of public confidence, money would lose its legitimacy. The government has designated currency as "legal tender." Paper currency is a liability of the government, and checks are a liability of commercial banks.

Confidence in these forms of money is also tied in some way to the fact that there are assets on the books of the government and the banks equal to the amount of money outstanding—even though nowadays most of these assets themselves are no more than pieces of paper. Government must, therefore, be sound and merit the full faith and confidence of the people. Unfortunately, we have come into a time of "fiat money"—which is unbacked or irredeemable paper that is declared to be legal tender by government edict. Surely, in an enlightened democratic society, the cynical remarks about government by Montesquieu no longer apply: "Then, again, the King is a great magician, for his dominion extends to the minds of his subjects; he makes them think what he wishes. If he has only a million crowns, he has only to persuade them that one crown is worth two, and they believe it."

The next chapter will discuss the sometime fate of fiat money, as we explore some "unlearned lessons from history." For now, let us tap two sources of wisdom for clues to the understanding of money. One is an older and the other is a contemporary voice. Both view fiat money with alarm and visions of disaster.

Professor George C. Edwards, who taught mathematics at the University of California in Berkeley, wrote a classic little book on *Money* in 1923. His work has been largely ignored then as now, despite his efforts for a hearing with government and banking authorities. Edwards spoke on behalf of "sound money" and was thoroughly opposed to fiat money, which he feared would become meaningless.

In fact, the good professor argued that credit is not money. It can only be "as if" money. In his view, money is that representative of *value* which is used as a medium of exchange. Most people define the value of money in terms of its purchasing power. Edwards would say that this puts the cart before the horse. "Money has purchasing power because of its value. It is not the purchasing power that gives it its value. If it did not have value, it would not have any purchasing power."[8]

Edwards was particularly critical of fiat paper money: "An issue of paper that is beyond the power of Government to redeem in gold or silver is fiat money and is not real money."[9] So long as there is fiat money, Edwards predicted that panic is invited, a panic that would be national and, ultimately, international. He warned that the abundant supply of paper money makes for easy virtue, and he feared that currency based on credit would point the way to bankruptcy. He was prescient in his observation that an inflated currency increases bank deposits which, in turn, makes the borrowing of money easier. Since this pushes prices up and up, there would be a temptation to print more money and press credit to the limit.

Edwards perceived a clear link between credit and inflation. When money is inflated it will be worth less until it becomes practically worthless. He deplored the excesses and extravagances, the hedonistic satisfaction with whims and fancies of high and loose living. In a passage that bears a contemporary ring, Edwards noted in 1923: "Demands for higher wages due to increased living costs, strikes, boycotts by housewives, investigations by Congress, and utterances of the President of the United States certainly indicate we are in financial turmoil."[10]

Obviously, times have not changed that much. Some might want to articulate Edwards's concerns in less moralistic tones, but there is righteous indignation properly being voiced. His conviction is simply that if money is built on a false premise, if there is no real intrinsic value to our paper money, then the whole thing could come tumbling down with a crash. He is correct in his estimation that the overissuing of paper money invites excessive spending at all levels from the individual to the government. He is also right in forging a link between the money supply and inflationary thrusts. Moreover, he is on target in believing that by piling up national debts the present generation is irresponsibly passing on to future generations obligations which it abdicates. This he finds morally reprehensible.

What Edwards underestimates is the role of confidence in sustaining the entire "as if" money system. My basic concern is that the economic and moral justification for this relationship of confidence is near the straining point. If public confidence continues to falter, then I would concede that Edwards's fears of an eventual monetary collapse are justified.

Next we turn to a contemporary monetary expert, John Exter, retired senior vice president of First National City Bank and former vice president of the Federal Reserve Bank of New York in charge of international banking. He, too, sees himself as a lonely prophet crying in the wilderness.

Exter has a tragic sense that the events of history are marching relentlessly toward a worldwide monetary collapse due to the wholesale substitution of paper money for commodity money, that is, paper money without the backing of gold. Paper money cut adrift from its moorings is completely undisciplined and knows no limits.

Exter differs strongly with the two reigning schools of economic theory—the Keynesians and the Friedmanites—in charging that both assume a "closed," or domestic, economy, whereas today's world of interdependency calls for a global perspective. Both schools are also oblivious to the enormous debt problem created by monetary expansion, which Exter regards as the clue to the coming collapse. Finally, both schools ignore the role of gold convertibility and advocate irredeemable paper money.

To John Exter, the crux of the problem is the lack of understanding of the functions that money serves.[11] Money is a means of payment, a standard of value, and a store of value. All three functions are important, but the store of value function is critical. Money that does not serve this task cannot ultimately survive. Because paper is far too abundant, it cannot serve as a good store of value. To be a good store of value, it must be scarce. And the only way to keep it scarce is to have it convertible into some scarce commodity—such as gold—at a fixed price. Only gold performs all three functions of money satisfactorily.

Incidentally, many economists and banking and governmental officials scoff at gold, ridiculing it as the "barbaric yellow metal." Yet, as an index of fear or of loss of confidence in paper currency, the value of gold on the world markets has zoomed upward and has been gyrating wildly. This remarkable activity began at the $41 level when Richard Nixon closed the gold window on August 15, 1971.

Since Nixon's attempt to demonetize gold, paper currencies are now being used to serve the three functions of money. None of these fiat currencies is adequate for the task. All are losing value in the marketplace day by day as inflation mounts.

Now the world is caught up in an unbridled growth of debt, the most dangerous segment being the voluminous Eurodollars, estimated by Morgan Guaranty Trust Co. at $965 billion as of mid-1979—or more than all the national bank deposits of the world's developed free-market countries. Until recently, these Eurodollars were free from any reserve requirements imposed by the Fed. They constitute "hot" and volatile money. Note that the former chairman of the Federal Reserve Board, G. William Miller, publicly recognized the possibility of a Eurodollar financial panic. The reason for his concern was the "danger that the Eurodollar market might possibly be vulnerable to a money panic. . . . A panic of the type of crisis that plagued 19th century financial markets is highly unlikely in modern domestic systems, but we don't know whether we could have one in the international field," notes Miller.[12]

Exter graphically pictures the world's financial system as an inverted pyramid of debt. In this upside-down view, the pinnacle becomes the base. This tiny base is gold—stored in central banks or under mattresses. Everything above that small base is paper money—a vast complex of IOUs, of debtor-creditor relationships of all sorts. The paper debtors above the gold base can be arrayed according to their relative degree of liquidity. The most liquid are located near the base, and the most illiquid at the very top. Of course, an inverted pyramid is a top-heavy structure.

As the pyramid grows, debt grows faster and faster, at an exponential rate. The entire worldwide financial system is riddled with debts that can no longer be paid by increased productivity. The only way this debt can be repaid is by creating still more debt. Inflation adds to the demand for credit and stimulates still further growth of the debt pyramid. We are locked into an expansionism that dare not be stopped, lest the entire system should collapse.

Exter recognizes that confidence does hold the system together and that there will come a point when this necessary confidence between debtor and creditor is ruptured. The illiquid debtors at the top of the pyramid will feel the squeeze most. Debt burden will become oppressive; failure will not be contained, and a domino effect or a snowballing of failures will follow. It will produce such a collapse of confidence that creditors in the debt pyramid will begin to flee the illiquid debtors at the top and move down into more liquid debtors toward the bottom of the pyramid. The scramble for liquidity will touch off a money panic. Deflation, following on the heels of inflation, will finally liquidate the debt excesses, and the pyramid will be set right side up. So goes the Exter scenario.

It is indeed tragic that so few are listening to the voice of this lonely prophet, John Exter. For he points to a fundamental flaw in our financial system, which encourages the excessive flow of paper money and the accumulation of debt at all levels of spending. In a later chapter we will contend that, ethically speaking, easy money in a world of shrinking resources leads to profligacy and illusory expectations.

A strange and eerie meaning is hidden in John Exter's choice of the pyramid as a metaphor of excessive illiquidity. At one time, the great pyramid at Cholulu in central Mexico, one of Mesoamerica's largest pyramids, must have been a sight of sheer aesthetic beauty and symmetry. Upon closer inspection, however, the real clue to understanding this pyramid was not as a work of art, but by what lay within—namely, a sacrificial platform. Here the gods were placated by a regular diet of human bodies as sacrificial offerings. According to the legend, if the gods were not fed regularly with human blood, the universe would fall apart. In fact, so many victims were lined up for sacrifice at the altar, it is speculated that the Aztec empire eventually collapsed under the oppressive weight of such genocidal human sacrifice.

The parabolic significance of the great pyramid of our neighbor to the south should be quite clear. Countless victims of the credit binge are being led to the altar of sacrifice. To placate the insatiable gods of consumerism, more and more victims will be necessary. Individuals, banks, cities, national governments come to the pyramid of sacrifice. Then, one day, the whole system will collapse of its own weight.

When that day of judgment will come and whether or for how long the day of reckoning can be deferred or postponed, no one knows for certain. Our faith informs us that this will not be the end of the world; rather a new creation—a new heaven and a new earth—is promised. Far from being the end of the world, the world will be coming to a new beginning!

The role of faith will be explored in the final chapter. Meanwhile, my motto is:

> *Prepare for the worst,*
> *Hope for the best;*
> *Get to work,*
> *Do something about the mess.*

IV

Unlearned Lessons
from History

In recent years Americans have looked longingly upon the German mark as a strong currency. In fact, some Americans have been anxious to unload their dollars in exchange for marks, thereby reversing Gresham's law and having "good" money drive out the bad. Indeed, as the dollar wavers and suffers its ups and downs, there is considerable discussion about its continued suitability as a "key currency." Some Europeans predict that a new currency system will emerge which is based on the German mark and will become the monetary and trading support of the world economy. The mark was not always such a favored currency.

Who has not played the children's game, "King of the Royal Mountain"? Recall that one player assumes a high place and announces kingship over the territory. Then other players attempt to invade the "mountain," displace the "king," and take over command. If the king is stronger than his competitors or rivals, he usually remains on top, enjoying his reign for a long time. Others may scheme and band together to remove him by force. Or some may strive to win the king's favor. Usually the king tires or grows bored and another girl or boy ascends to the throne.

While not to be taken too literally, children's games frequently bear close resemblance to adult socio-geo-political situations. In a sense, the monetary world is a stage where a grandiose game of "King of the Royal Mountain" is being played—for keeps!

A cursory glance at history should remind us of the relative strength of the dollar and the mark in the early 1920s. German inflation was forging ahead at a dizzying pace in a runaway economy. Before World War I, the mark was worth 23.82 cents, to the dollar. In 1923, the mark went to the astronomical sum of 16 trillion to the dollar, before it eventually stabilized at a mere 4 trillion.

Postwar Germany was filled with social and political upheaval. Enormous reparations were exacted by the Allies after the First World War. A drastic decline in production and the progressive increase in the issuance of paper currency contributed to the chaos. With raging inflation rates, the value of the paper money was constantly tumbling.

By the fall of 1925, the German mark exploded, so that all the marks in the world (190 billion of them) were not worth enough to purchase a single newspaper or train ticket. It was a spectacular collapse that had been preceded by persisting inflation over a nine-year period. During the inflationary phase, Germany experienced economic boom, hefty profits, high rates of consumer spending, securities speculation—all fueled by excessive debt and credit. At the onset of World War I in the summer of 1914, Germany abandoned its gold standard, began running large budget deficits, expanded its money supply, and covered its war-born deficits with loans and issues of new paper reichsmarks.

Between 1914 and 1918, domestic prices more than doubled, while the government's money supply increased by nine times. After the war, the German economy continued to inflate and enjoyed a remarkable boom. While most of the other combatant nations (including the United States) went through a serious recession, Germany was the envy of other countries because of its amazing postwar prosperity. Of course the boom of 1920–1921 was fueled by the government's easy money policy, by deficit expenditures, and by overextension of credit. Industry and business were advancing at fever pitch. Profits were healthy and unemployment virtually nil. Exports were thriving. Speculation was rife, as the allure to make a quick killing in the stock market became well-nigh irresistable. Trading volume reached such heights that the German bourse, or stock exchange, was obliged to close several days a week in order to work off its office backlog. Cabaret life was celebrated, as Berlin became a glittering world capital. Acquisitions, mergers, tender offers, and conglomerate empires were the rage of the day. Prosperity was in the air. Frugality was replaced by prodigality. Then the collapse came with a vengeance.

As the inflationary boom peaked, a sudden descent carried the economy plunging downward. From July to October, 1921, prices doubled. They continued to climb. Interest rates soared, reaching as high as 22% per day. Government debt could not be refinanced except by printing additional paper money. By July, 1922, prices had risen tenfold in four months, and then they really exploded by an astonishing two-hundred-fold in the next eleven months. By the end of 1923, prices were quadrupling each week.

Confidence in the value of money was completely sapped. Instead of conducting a futile boycott, as in the earlier days of the inflationary binge, consumers were now avidly competing among themselves to buy up goods before their money evaporated. When the boom expired, farmers would not sell their products to city dwellers for their worthless paper currency. Production fell drastically, factories closed their doors, small businesses were swept away, and rates of unemployment and starvation skyrocketed. Food riots ensued. As many as 85 people were killed in one such riot in Hamburg.

Single mark notes of one-billion denomination were printed in the Germany of 1923. Those who lived through the experience can still remember needing a briefcase full of paper money just to ride the street car. A pickpocket in those days would do better stealing the briefcase than the currency within! German housewives were known to have rushed to the factory gates to draw their husbands' pay twice a day to spend it immediately for goods before its purchasing power was eroded further. With the currency depreciating day by day, even from hour to hour, the only value it possessed was gained by hurrying to the market and spending it. The depreciation of paper money in Germany dealt a severe blow to low and middle income persons, who felt its impact for years to come.

By mid-1923, currency stabilization had returned with the issue of a new and strictly limited supply of rentenmarks, which replaced the old reichmarks on a one-trillion reichsmark to one rentenmark ratio. A year later, still reeling from the shock waves of financial disruption, the German people voted by the millions for either the Communist or the Nazi party. Although the moderate political parties prevailed that time, the election served as a warning signal of the storm brewing over the horizon. With the Depression of 1929, debtor Germany was knocked flat on its back again. These unstable conditions provided the soil for the emergence of Adolf Hitler, who eventually assumed power on January 31, 1933, as the leader of the National Socialist Party.

During this same period, France also experienced financial instability, turning to heavy borrowing and the ubiquitous printing press. At the end of World War I, France issued more than 27 billion francs. This sum mounted to 38 billion in 1920. The franc narrowly escaped going the way of the German mark. Finally in 1926, a devaluation of 80% was declared by the French government. The bankruptcy of Germany in 1923 and the narrow escape of France from a similar fate in 1926 were ominous harbingers of the world economic depression that began in 1929.

Economic collapse, following an inflationary spiral that was exacerbated by a flood of printing-press money, has been seen again and again in history. Disraeli once said, "Confidence is suspicion asleep." Suppose suspicion should awaken from its deep slumber? Then what? Will confidence take flight?

Historical crises cannot be oversimplified by single-cause explanations. Indeed, social causation is complex and must be viewed in the matrix of a constellation of factors. The case may be made, however, that there has been insufficient attention given to the erosion of public confidence in the aftermath of the surging supply of fiat money as a significant source of economic collapse.

We have only to point to the lessons of history: in France between 1716 and 1720, under the reckless, experimental schemes of John Law, and again during the revolutionary period of 1791–1796; with the experience of the French currency assignats; in our own experience with our Continental currency between 1775 and 1780 and the Greenbacks during the Civil War; in the German inflation of the 1920s; in China after World War II; and in various Latin American nations, such as Peru, Argentina, and Chile.

Of course, in each case there were extenuating circumstances. In the case of our Continental currency, for instance, one of the main reasons it suffered was the boat loads of counterfeit Continental currency shipped from England. The wily British used the currency to flood the market in the Colonies as a weapon of war.

Perhaps students of monetary history claim too much for the correlation between a debased currency and the fall of a nation. However, one's attention is certainly arrested by the dictum of Antonius Augustus: "Money has more to do with the distemper of the Roman Empire than the Huns and the Vandals." Historian George Finlay comments on the fall of the Roman Empire as follows:

> In reviewing the causes which contributed to the decline of the wealth and dimunution of the population of the Roman Empire, it is necessary to take into account the depreciation of the coinage, which frequently robbed large classes of the industrious citizens of a great part of their wealth, reduced the value of property, produced confusion in legal contracts, and anarchy in prices in the public markets. The evils which must have resulted from the enormous depreciation of the Roman coinage at several periods

can only be understood . . . by remembering that each issue of a depreciated coinage was an act of bankruptcy on the part of a reigning emperor.[13]

A reading of the classic primer by historian-diplomat Andrew Dickson White, the first president of Cornell University, on the fate of the French fiat paper currency known as the assignat is a sobering experience. One cannot appreciate the full force of the monetary and political crisis without some understanding of the French Revolution and its political chronology:

CHRONOLOGICAL TABLE[14]

	1789	*Assignats in circulation (millions of livres or francs)*
MAY 5	An attempt to cure the bankrupt state of the public treasury caused Louis XVI to call a meeting of the States-General, which later amalgamated into the single-chamber National Assembly	
JULY 14	Fall of the Bastille, after several days of rioting in Paris	
OCTOBER 5	Declaration of the Rights of Man adopted by Assembly	
NOVEMBER 2	Confiscation of Church property	

	1790	
APRIL	First issue of paper assignats, 400 million livres	400
SEPTEMBER 29	Second issue, 800 million	1,200

	1791	
JUNE 19	Third issue, 600 million	1,800
SEPTEMBER	New Constitution; National Assembly dissolved and replaced by Legislative Assembly	
DECEMBER 17	Fourth issue, 300 million	2,100

	1792	Assignats in circulation (millions of livres or francs)
APRIL 30	Fifth issue, 300 million France at war with Russia and Austria	2,400
JUNE-AUGUST	Riots in Paris; King dethroned and royal family imprisoned; Revolutionary Commune takes power; more assignats	2,700
SEPTEMBER	Election of National Convention replacing Legislative Assembly; Monarchy abolished; government by committees; political corruption	
DECEMBER 14	Total assignats issued to date 3,400 million; 600 million destroyed	2,800

	1793	
JANUARY 21	Louis XVI beheaded	
JANUARY 31	More assignats	3,000
FEBRUARY-MARCH	Formation of Committee of Public Safety; rioting in Paris over high prices; Revolutionary Tribunal established; Reign of Terror begins	
MAY 3	Price control on grains	
JUNE 22	Forced Loan decreed—a progressive income tax	
AUGUST 1	Trading in specie prohibited	
SEPTEMBER 29	Law of the Maximum—price control extended to all food	
OCTOBER 16	Marie Antoinette beheaded—Over 3,000 million new assignats issued during the year, of which 1,200 million entered circulation	4,200

	1794	
JUNE 4	Robespierre elected president of National Convention; thousands executed by decree of Revolutionary Tribunal	

JULY 27	Robespierre beheaded; end of Reign of Terror	
DECEMBER	Law of Maximum repealed	
	Assignats in circulation at end of year	7,000

1795

MAY 31	Assignats in circulation	
	More rioting; business and trade disrupted; shortages persist; uncertain government	14,000
JULY 31	Assignats in circulation	14,000
SEPTEMBER 23	New Constitution adopted and new government formed—the Directory	35,000

1796

FEBRUARY 18	Machinery, plates, and paper for printing assignats destroyed	
	First issue of new paper notes—mandats—to displace assignats at 30:1	40,000
AUGUST	Mandats worth only 3 per cent of face value; about 2,500 million mandats issued altogether	

1797

FEBRUARY	Legal tender qualities withdrawn from both assignats and mandats, which became worthless after May

1798

	Arbitrary government by the Directory; business disrupted; people discontented; Napoleon gaining military victories abroad

1799

NOVEMBER 10	Napoleon comes into power—"to save the Republic"

A cursory glance at this chronology reveals the interplay between political and economic developments. It is not simply that political instability and terror led to monetary chaos. Runaway inflation brought wealth to some and anguish for many. A new luxury class emerged, while the burdens on underpaid laborers were oppressive. The resulting envy, alienation, and discontent fueled the flames of political upheaval and violence.

Because the public treasury was bankrupt, inflation was begun in revolutionary France to pay off debt and to finance a budget deficit. The remedy to overcome the shortage of funds was to add to the circulating medium by printing assignats in order to produce more purchasing power. As results were not immediately beneficial, then more and more assignats were printed.

The printing of more paper money was viewed as a "short road to prosperity," a way of "securing resources without paying interest," so went the public outcry. Despite the fact that only 70 years earlier John Law had taken France down a dismal path of financial disaster with his paper money scheme, it was argued that this time a constitutional government controlled by an enlightened, patriotic people could handle successfully the new issue of irredeemable paper money.

The assignat was even backed by claims against church properties, which were confiscated to serve this purpose, and it also bore interest at 3% to the holder. A vast sum of 400 million assignats was initially printed. There was immediate relief and rejoicing as a portion of the public debt was paid. Creditors were encouraged, credit revived, trade increased, and the economy seemed to be moving forward again. Five months later, when the government had spent its funds and unrest grew, there was a clamor for another issue of paper money. To "save the country," this time 800 million new assignats were issued along with the announcement that the revolution was now completed, save for a few minor details.

Prices continued to rise, as the new issue of paper was merely a drop of cold water to a parched throat. The cry for "more circulating medium" persisted, and the supply was still further increased to meet the insatiable demand. In full force was the doctrine that all currency derives its efficacy from the official stamp it bears. This being the case, a government may relieve itself of its debts simply by printing more fiat money.

Despite cries from saner voices that the continuing increase of paper money would lead to ruin, the process was repeated again and again. Inflation was erroneously confused with prosperity. The greater the amount of paper money printed, the more specie (coin or gold) disappeared from view. Those who hoarded gold were condemned as wicked and unpatriotic citizens. The revolutionary leader Marat asserted that death was the appropriate punishment for gold hoarders.

Stagflation set in as prices continued to rise, but business languished. The earlier stimulus to trade and enterprise now gave way to business contraction and ultimate collapse. A political leader of the period noted: " 'Commerce was dead; betting took its place.' "[15] Speculation and gambling were widespread as moneymaking schemes circulated wildly.

White describes in detail how, with every new printing of fiat money, economic and moral laxity were engendered among the populace with disastrous consequences:

> One of these was the *obliteration of thrift* from the minds of the French people. The French are naturally thrifty; but, with such masses of money and with such uncertainty as to its future value, the ordinary motives for saving and care diminished, and a loose luxury spread throughout the country.
>
> A still worse outgrowth was the increase in speculation and gambling. With the plethora of paper currency in 1791 appeared the first evidences of that cancerous disease which always follows large issues of irredeemable currency. . . . In the country at large there grew a dislike of steady labor and a contempt for moderate gains and simple living.[16]

In the bitter end, 40 thousand million francs were issued. So great was the demand that the small army of engravers and printers could not produce the amount desired. The purchasing power of the assignat dwindled to almost nothing. Finally, on

December 22, 1795, it was decreed that the copper plates should be broken and the paper for printing assignats burned.

Fiat money inflation in France brought with it widespread distrust, cynicism, and the erosion of personal faith and public confidence. Without confidence in the future, few dared to make business investments. It was considered folly to curtail the pleasures of the moment or to save for prospects so uncertain and precarious.

Paper money drifted more and more into the hands of the working class, employees, and persons of smaller means; members of the wealthier class were shrewd enough to rid themselves of paper currency for objects of permanent value. Thus, a thrifty hardware merchant retired from business in 1790 with 321,000 livres, or francs. In 1796, when the tide of inflation had ebbed, this man had just 14,000 francs left. Approximately 29/30th's of his savings had evaporated.

Such was the fate of fiat money in revolutionary France, when an attempt was made to cure a debt disease with a remedy that was worse than the original malady in its consequences. The "law of accelerating issue and depreciation" was in full force: The more paper currency is issued, the less its worth becomes. Whether or not there are ominous parallels between 18th-century France and 20th-century America and lessons to be learned will be left for the discriminating reader to judge.

The German and French experiences with fiat money lead me to the conclusion that fiat money is only as sound as its source, only as valid as the sovereignty that issues it. Ultimately, fiat money is as stable as its acceptability by the people and their confidence in the currency.

Returning to our nation's own economic holocaust, it may be instructive to compare our present period with the Roaring Twenties that culminated in the Great Crash of 1929.

Then, as now, inflation increased at a galloping rate. Steadily rising prices were fueled then, as now, by credit extension. Then, as now, there was a large increase in private debt. The policy of easy availability of credit was begun in 1927 by the

Federal Reserve Board of New York. Ironically, the policy was instigated following a visit by the governors of European central banks, who made the plea that unless the United States adopted an easy credit policy, there would be economic collapse in Europe. The ill-fated policy was pursued to avert worldwide economic collapse. Hence, overall debt increased markedly until the brakes were slammed on in 1929.

Then—but not yet now—there was a loss of confidence by the public in the banking system. In reviewing the pre-Depression period, an eminent scholar on the history of the monetary experience concludes: "Under the conditions that grew up around a situation of constantly expanding banking operations based on steadily diminishing reserves, it was inevitable that a crash should occur. . . . The stupendous house of banking had been built upon sand—public confidence in the infallibility and capacity of the institution—and when the sand began to shift, the whole structure toppled like an Egyptian monolith."[17]

Then—but not yet now—confidence sagged in the business community, so that investments by businesses were at a standstill, resulting in the Keynesian metaphor of the stuck elevator. Jobs became scarce, and people were thrown out of work until the unemployment rate soared to 25% of the population. The spiral continued: Unemployed people cannot afford to buy goods, forcing businesses to cut back further, throwing even more people out of work, etc.

Consider also that in the crash of 1929, the brokers' loans to customers for stock purchases on margin had increased alarmingly:

> June, 1922   . . . $1.7 billion
> December, 1926 . . . $3.3 billion
> December, 1927 . . . $4.4 billion
> December, 1928 . . . $6.4 billion
> September, 1929 . . . $8.5 billion
> December, 1932 . . . $0.3 billion

Until the crash, stocks were purchased with borrowed money, the buyer needing to put up only 10 to 20% cash. Overspeculation was encouraged, as market plungers sought to make a "quick killing." When the market plummeted, lending institutions had to sell their customers' stocks to protect their loans. Note that by September of 1929—just prior to the crash—the amount of borrowed funds had increased to a peak of $8.5 billion, almost double the 1927 figure of $4.4 billion.

By late summer, 1979, the figure for stock purchases on margin stood at $12 billion—the highest in recorded history. Although high on a numerical basis, however, these recent margin figures are not as alarming on a percentage basis when compared to 1929. Margin requirements are now 50% in contrast to the 10% that prevailed in 1929. Nowadays speculation and leverage are more evident in the real-estate market than in stocks. Under the "greater fool theory," home buyers realize that the prices they pay are exorbitant, but surely some greater fool will buy from them at even more inflated prices. At some point, of course, the bubble bursts.

To return to the devastation of 1929, on October 24 there were 12,894,650 shares of stock traded on the New York Stock Exchange amid scenes of wild panic. On that day, shares of General Electric dropped 47 points, Westinghouse fell 34½, and Allied Chemical, 36. On October 29 the market sank still further, with 16,410,030 shares being sold. By year's end, more than $40 billion had been deflated from the value of New York Stock Exchange securities. Now, of course, these trading figures would make for dull days indeed, as the New York Stock Exchange averaged 30 million shares per day during 1979. A really big day saw 55 or 60 million shares exchanged, with the record being nearly 82 million.

A sarcastic ditty, which is appropriate for the days of the crash of '29, goes as follows:

> *On Monday I bought share on share;*
> *On Tuesday I was a millionaire;*
> *On Wednesday took a grand abode;*
> *On Thursday in my carriage rode;*
> *On Friday drove to the opera ball;*
> *On Saturday came to the pauper's hall.*

In his classic analysis *The Great Crash, 1929,* John Kenneth Galbraith notes that the essential difference between the October, 1929, debacle and earlier market declines was that previous troubles happened and were suddenly over. However, during the crash, the worst continued to worsen.[18] What looked like an end to troubles proved only to have been the beginning. Westinghouse had been trading at 286 on September 3; on October 29, it opened at 130 and promptly dropped to 100. Goldman Sachs Trading Corporation fell from 60 to 35 in a single day. In September, 1929, Blue Ridge traded at 24; on October 29, it sank to 3. So stunning were the slumps in share prices that the days ran out of invidious labels, such as "Black Thursday," "Blue Monday," "Terrible Tuesday." Each day the dark canyons of lower Manhattan seemed to grow darker. As a leading journal of the day expressed it, "Stocks were selling not ex-dividend, but ex-hope and ex-romance."[19]

The feverish slide continued as Otis Elevator lost 45 points and Auburn Automobile skidded 66 points on November 5. U.S. Steel slumped a mere 16 points on that dark day. All through the next week the declines continued to worsen, as exaggerated stories of suicide jumps from high windows spread across the land. Although on the macabre side, humor abounded. Hotel clerks reportedly asked guests whether they wished the room for sleeping or jumping.

From October, 1929, to November 13, the Times Industrial Index showed a drastic drop from 452 down to 224. If this seemed nightmarish, note that by July 8, 1932, the Times Industrial Index had sunk to 58. On that day, U.S. Steel hit a low of 22 from its pre-crash days of 262. General Motors was a mere 8, down from 73. Montgomery Ward fell to 4, down from 138. Anaconda sold at 4. Our previously cited Blue Ridge was now worth only 63¢. American Founders was selling at 50¢ as compared to an earlier price of 117. Needless to say, Wall Street was suffering from a total collapse of confidence. Quite a contrast from the euphoric pre-crash days when the eminent Yale economist Professor Irving Fisher could claim that "stocks have reached what appears to be a permanently high plateau!"[20]

The widely quoted Dow Jones Industrial Average reached a peak of 386 on September 3, 1929. By July 8, 1932, the precipitous slide finally bottomed out at 41—a collapse of 89%. Dow Jones was not to climb back to its pre-crash level again for 25 years.

The companies that dropped the most drastically—down to almost nothing—were those that were highly leveraged, that had been operating excessively on borrowed funds. In the heyday of prosperity—then as now—it seemed conventionally wise to borrow heavily, to maximize profit gains by using other people's money. As Galbraith noted: "The investment trusts, once considered a buttress of the high plateau and a built-in defense against collapse, were really a profound source of weakness. The leverage, of which people only a fortnight before had spoken so knowingly and even affectionately, was now fully in reverse. With remarkable celerity, it removed all of the value from the common stock of a trust."[21] Leverage, alas, is always a two-way street.

All through the early months following the October stock market crash, political and business leaders, such as President Herbert Hoover, Rockefeller, and Ford, were reassuring the public that equity prices were "historically cheap." In a rare public statement from Pocantico Hills, John D. Rockefeller stated: "Believing that fundamental conditions of the country are sound . . . my sons and I have for some days been purchasing sound common stocks." In response, comedian Eddie Cantor was quick to quip: "Sure, who else had any money left?"[22]

In any case, the pep talks by prominent leaders failed to support equity prices, which became historically even cheaper. President Hoover turned to the familiar tactic of calling a series of meetings with industrialists and other leading citizens invited to the White House in an orchestrated attempt to restore confidence, which Galbraith referred to as "organized reassurance on a really grand scale."[23] Repeated reassurances that the Depression would soon be over, that imminent prosperity was at hand, and a flood of optimistic forecasts had little connection with reality. They sounded strangely similar to the reassurances issued by government officials during the agonizing years of the Vietnam War declaring that the conflict would soon be drawing to a rapid close.

All the orchestrated and organized "confidence" by leaders of the world of finance and politics failed to stem the tide, as the flood of panic selling continued. The Great Depression shook up the entire credit structure of the American economy. Beginning with the stock market crash that lasted nearly uninterrupted for two years, the Depression saw a severe cut in the volume of business, the ebbing of sales, the decline of corporate profits, rising rates of unemployment, and disruption of the banking system. Although the unemployment rate was 25% nationwide, in some communities it reached as high as 60%. As a result, the Great Depression dealt a blow to the traditional American work ethic (to be reviewed in a later chapter), which held that hard work is rewarded by success and good fortune. Unemployment caught up in its vast net both the energetic and the feckless, the virtuous and the irresponsible. All the accumulated excesses ran through their painful course, as the economy found itself trapped in a spiraling downward tailspin.

One final caveat about the Great Depression—The Ryan Report of debts incurred by consumers showed the shift in American buying habits leading up to crash:

ITEM: In 1925, with retail sales of $53 billion, sales on credit had increased to $18 billion. From 1925 to 1930, the credit increased more heavily. In 1930, retail sales were $60 billion, and sales on credit $30 billion. Between 1925 and 1930, therefore, the proportion of sales made on credit rose from 34% to 50% of total sales.

Ryan concluded that 50 years before, no one would have dreamed that our once predominantly thrifty, cash-basis populace would by 1929 and 1930 become not thrifty at all. "No one would have predicted in those days, when most people never got into debt and always lived within their means, that in 1929, 1930, nearly every American family would be in debt."[24] Extensive investigations by Ryan in 1928–1930 indicate that during that period 98% of American families were indebted in some way or other.

If Ryan was astonished by the amount of consumer debts incurred just prior to the Great Crash, he would be absolutely horrified by the figures related in our earlier chapter on consumer debts. These debts have grown much more rapidly in recent years than in the late 1920s! The excessive debt load now weighs like the burden of Atlas on the shoulders of our economy.

Just prior to the crash of '29, the signs of boom and prosperity were highly visible: a bull market in stocks, increasing commodity prices, and an explosively upside real-estate market. The next phase is history. Those who claim that there could never be another crash comparable to the calamity of 1929–1932 best not ignore the danger signals inherent in the present-day debt and credit binge, which surely make our economy vulnerable.

Several additional caveats from history are worth noting. These pertain to the status and possible role of religion during the Great Depression in America. It is commonly assumed that a "bust" in the economy would result in a boom in religion. After all, goes the argument, if people are afflicted by adversity, deep in despair, they will naturally seek out churches for strength, solace, and spiritual sustenance. Crisis is a sure summons to return to fundamental virtues and values. If it works in the foxholes during wartime, it must also apply to the hard times of economic adversity.

Despite the anxiety and perplexity encountered during the 1930s and contrary to popular assumptions, there was no great return to religion. People were simply not stampeding to darken the doors of churches. The most reliable studies, by Sam Kincheloe of the University of Chicago (conducted during the Depression with WPA funds) and by Robert T. Handy of Union Theological Seminary, indicate that no significant increase either in church membership or attendance was discernible.[25]

The only significant growth was found among emotional, sectarian groups, such as the Nazarenes, Holiness groups, and Pentecostals, which began with a small base in numbers. But even here, growth was largely confined to the southeastern sector of the nation. What actually happened was that the churches—especially mainline Protestantism—were considerably weakened by the Depression. Financial giving by the membership to sustain benevolences, missionary endeavors, and national denominational offices was drastically curtailed. Budgets were slashed by 50% in a single year. In fact, 20 of the 35 leading denominations cut their budgets from 30 to 50% in the year 1934, while 5 groups were forced to trim more than 50%. Organizationally speaking, the churches were rendered too weak to respond with energy and resources as the great knife of Depression cut deeply into their life and work.

The outcome of the Great Depression was to break the stronghold of Protestantism upon American culture. No longer the "custodian of the faith," Protestantism came out of the Depression dethroned. It ceased to be *the* dominant religious tradition; it had lost its cultural hegemony. Prior to the Depression, in 1927, the astute French author André Siegfried could claim that " 'the civilization of the United States is essentially Protestant' and 'Protestantism is the only national religion.' "[26] This state of affairs was drastically altered by the Great Depression.

The shattering of Protestant power paved the way for the religious pluralism that we celebrate today. Were it not for the Depression's impact, one wonders if the election of a Roman Catholic president—John F. Kennedy—could have become a historical reality. Contrast the election campaign of Catholic candidate Alfred E. Smith in 1928, when the religious issue was one among other burning points raised, and old fears of Romanism were stirred. Note that while campaigning for the presidency, John F. Kennedy took pains to disassociate himself from the Pope. Nowadays, a born-again Baptist president can joyously host a Pope in the White House for the first time in American history, and invitations for the gala affair are highly prized! The Great Depression fundamentally altered not simply the landscape of American politics and economic policy, but also the configuration of religious institutions.

One further bombshell lesson from the Great Depression is noted by the gifted American church historian Robert T. Handy: There was a distinct and separate religious depression that occurred in the mid-1920s prior to the economic setback of the '30s. By the middle of the 1920s, a spiritual decline had engulfed the churches. A bitter fundamentalist vs. modernist controversy lowered the general prestige of religion and also sapped the enthusiasm and commitment of many church members. Missionary giving fell sharply—at a time of general economic prosperity—and missionary zeal was waning.

Handy documents the data of a prior religious depression in the foreign and home mission movements, in the demise of the Inter Church World Movement, in the lowered status of ministers in public esteem, in the low morale that gripped the churches following the post-war period, in the popularity of humanism, in the pervasive spirit of lethargy, and in the debunking of faith by prominent literary figures such as Sinclair Lewis and H. L. Mencken. In short, there was a spiritual depression, an internal Protestant depression, in advance of the coming economic impoverishment.

As a historian, Handy sought to draw a clear distinction between the religious depression in the twenties and the economic depression that followed in the thirties. Though unintended by Handy, his careful scholarship has provided me with a bold and provocative hypothesis. It is bound to be criticized from all quarters—but, alas, such is the nature of brash hypotheses: If the religious depression preceded the economic depression the last time around, is there not predictive or foreshadowing power in this insight for the fire next time?

A religious depression may, indeed, presage an economic one. After all, a religious depression entails an erosion of confidence in the primacy of faith, a pervasive mood of spiritual ennui, a loss of morale (and morals) among former adherents to the faith. If God cannot be trusted, why should men and women trust mere mortals—political leaders and economic wizards? Why, indeed, should paper money be trusted—despite its claim "In God We Trust"—if the divine dimension in life is deflated? What begins as a loss of confidence in religion has a ripple effect and extends into the economic realm, so that religion and economic motives are inextricably intertwined.

Why shouldn't this idea be plausible? I can already hear a chorus of dissent, issuing from those who suffer from tunnel vision: the Marxian dialectical materialists who argue that the material substructure alters the ideational superstructure, and not the other way around, and the micro-econometric plodders and technical historians who argue for myriad complexities and multivariate analyses of historical causality.

Now, the burning question for next time. What evidence is there of a recent religious depression? Recall that the early seventies was a low point for religious institutions. In 1970 the National Protestant Episcopal Church slashed the professional staff of its executive council from 203 to 104 officers. Similar cuts in the name of reorganization of structures occurred in the United Presbyterian Church. As a result, hundreds of church bureaucrats suddenly discovered they were leaders without troops to lead. Virtually all the mainline Protestant denominations were slashing budgets and personnel. Seminary mergers or closures occurred, as budgets were cut, squeezed, and trimmed. Those without tenure wondered where the ax would fall next. Morale sagged along with membership and benevolence giving in the mainline churches. Finally, there was a "Death-of-God" movement, which happily died itself, or, rather, just petered out. A number of its apostles were advertising in secular journals for teaching positions. Churches wrangled over such issues as Angela Davis and Saul Alinsky's style of community organization.

It is true that organized religion has experienced a rebound since the early seventies, and many cultic groups, surrogate faiths, evangelistic-media religions have emerged. But then, recall that the recession of 1974 was said to be the worse downturn since the 1930s, especially painful around the wailing wall known as Wall Street, which witnessed the horrendous erosion of $300 billion in stock-market valuations.

Was 1974 the response to the "religious depression" of the early 1970s? Or are we to await something more cataclysmic in the 1980s?

Surely the followers of the Russian economist Nikolai D. Kondratieff are keeping a watchful and wary eye on the early 1980s. Who is this Kondratieff with his talk about "wave theories"? While not an American household name, Kondratieff and his theory are receiving more attention, as we enter the uncharted decade of the eighties. Formerly head of the Business Research Institute of Moscow, Kondratieff was a Russian economist during the Stalinist era. In 1930 he was arrested, exiled, imprisoned, and finally executed in Siberia for his heretical economic ideas. He could not subscribe to the party line that capitalism contains the seeds of its own destruction. Instead, in a series of books and articles published between 1922 and 1928, he viewed capitalism as going through business cycles of prosperity and poverty. He charted the ups and downs of capitalism from the beginning of the Industrial Revolution through the year 2000.[27] Indeed, Kondratieff was an early futurist, before that art became fashionable.

Kondratieff's research is not totally unknown in American economic circles. Noted Harvard economist Joseph A. Schumpeter relied on Kondratieff's work in his massive study *Business Cycles.* Former advisor to Lyndon Johnson's administration and economic scholar W. W. Rostow has also used Kondratieff's theories in his own studies of the stages of economic growth.

Kondratieff's painstaking research revealed that there were super cycles that come every 50 years or so, give or take 5 years. He could spot long waves of economic expansion and contraction. According to his super-wave theory, there has been and will continue to be a major economic depression every 50 years or so. The skeptical reader should test this theory and see what happens.

If you go back 50 years from 1929, sure enough, there was the serious depression of 1875.[28] Carry that back another 50 years or so, and again, look at the major depression of 1825. Now, projecting ahead from 1929 gives you the year 1979!

Perhaps Paul Erdman had Kondratieff in mind when he titled his spinetingling novel *The Crash of '79,* which smacks of considerable reality, though the book is presented in the guise of fiction. Many Kondratieff followers, such as Donald Hoppe, emphasize 52 or 54 years as the Kondratieff super-cycle. That brings us, of course, to the years 1981 and 1983!

All right, I have mixed feelings about such approaches myself. I resist playing numerology games, and I object to a mechanical view that renders human beings mere puppets on the stage of life. Somehow this sort of analysis does not fit my Calvinist temperament—although it is compatible with my Asian roots! However, I would not go so far as to say that Kondratieff —who courageously "took the hemlock" rather than give in to orthodoxy—is stupid or deserved his fate as an economic heretic. Surely Kondratieff's research is a far sight better than the eminent Professor Jevons's explanations of business cycles as caused by sunspots. And it also beats the insights coming from the popular Ouija board. Brash as I may appear, I am forced to look at the evidence of the unlearned lessons from history.

"Those who refuse to learn from history are doomed to repeat its failures," stated Santayana in an oft-repeated, but seldom honored aphorism. Despite all the comforts and blessings that money has conferred upon human beings, the use and abuse of money remains a problem that plagues individuals and governments alike. The perennial temptation is to take shortcuts to prosperity, to lust for easy profits, to satisfy immediate goals at the expense of long-range solutions.

To take a historical perspective—while not a comforting exercise—surely warns us of traps and snares into which wellmeaning and even intelligent persons have fallen. Could their mistakes have been avoided? Or is the nature of human nature such that we must commit the same follies given similar historical exigencies?

On the matter of credit inflation and fiat money, there is ample evidence to suggest that we follow the same lock-step responses, despite the tragic consequences we have witnessed throughout human history. We have seen the catastrophic results of highly inflationary policies in the past, both in the United States and elsewhere.

It is said that the fish is the last one to know that it is immersed in water. The early stages of inflation are accompanied by a similar sense of blissful ignorance. Many view inflation as beneficial, bringing greater prosperity, higher levels of employment, and larger incomes. Concerns about rising prices are dispelled by official pronouncements that inflation would soon be checked. An inflation "fighter" is appointed. At the next stage, there is growing awareness that one could gain by borrowing more to buy commodities and equipment, because currency depreciates much more rapidly than do tangible assets. During this phase, debt is liquidated by currency depreciation. If the outstanding debt is $3 trillion, for example, an average price increase of 10% a year would liquidate $300 billion of real debt. The need for more money grows, and government officials cannot resist the clamor. Additional funds are injected into the monetary system. Each injection creates more distortions. Eventually the final phase of runaway inflation is reached. People wake up to the recognition that their money is worth less and begin to flee the paper currency. A breakdown in public confidence brings the economy to the abyss of collapse.

In the past, inflationary policies have led to a breech of confidence in the value of money and a massive collapse in financial assets. It has led to stagflation, devaluations, and high unemployment. To embark on the course of reflation is to disregard the experiences learned so painfully in the lessons of human history.

The warning flags are up! The risks are serious! Hyper-inflation is an up-the-down-staircase experience. What goes up at first leads to the downward course towards collapse.

Already many Americans who have overextended their credit and cannot meet their debt obligations are being forced into bankruptcy. We shall explore this experience in all of its pain and poignancy in the next chapter.

V

Bankruptcy
and the
American Way of Debt

O Judge, the father of mischief,
  have mercy upon us miserable debtors.
O Secretary, recorder of wrongs,
  have mercy upon us miserable debtors.
O Marshal, confiner of persons and divider of families,
  have mercy upon us miserable debtors. [29]

This debtor's litany from the year 1800 is a supplication before a court of law, a plea for mercy by a contrite debtor. Today, we no longer have to beseech the court for mercy. Debtors have legal recourse and may resort to an institutionalized procedure in declaring bankruptcy that falls far short of begging for mercy.

In earlier annals of civilization, the power of creditors over delinquent or defaulted debtors led to cruel and inhuman punishment—including dismembering the body and distributing its parts to creditors, captivity, debtor's prisons, servitude, and the abuse of the body of the debtor or spouse with impunity.

The first bankruptcy laws were enacted in England in 1542. Through the centuries, bankruptcy laws generally have favored the creditors and protected their rights. Creditors could throw a debtor into jail and divide up among themselves the debtor's assets. Debtors did not have the right to declare bankruptcy voluntarily to relieve themselves of their debt obligations.

In the American experience, bankruptcy laws were incorporated into the U.S. Constitution (Article I, Section 8), and major legislation was enacted in 1800, 1841, 1867, 1898, and 1938. In an effort to suppress fraud and criminal practices, the Bankruptcy Act of 1800 was designed against debtors. Modeled after English laws, that act was repealed in 1803 because it gave governmental authorities excessive power. The Bankruptcy Act of 1898, amended several times, has long governed bankruptcy proceedings in this country. Its last major overhaul was the Chandler Act of 1938, which dealt with problems arising from the Depression. In 1979 the Congress enacted legislation to streamline and simplify bankruptcy proceedings. The new legislation allows more exemptions and invalidates certain liens on household goods. It is fair to say that legislation has increasingly shifted from protecting the rights of creditors to insuring the rights of debtors.

Bankruptcy laws function to relieve a person who is financially overextended and to provide an equitable way to distribute the available funds or assets to the creditors. Its intent is to show compassion to the honest debtor, to afford an opportunity for a fresh start, and to offer new hope.

To trace the legal history of bankruptcy is fascinating, but beyond our immediate scope. Nor do I want to get bogged down in the intricate details of bankruptcy proceedings—petitions, filings, schedules, exemptions, garnishments, trustees, lawyers, etc. The intention of this chapter is, rather, to focus on the human dimensions—the personal dramas and coping measures. Even though begging for mercy is unnecessary nowadays, there still exists considerable misery connected with bankruptcy. In this discussion I also want to indicate the scope of the American way of debt that can lead down the path to bankruptcy.

Personal Bankruptcy

I will present a detailed, real-life case history of bankruptcy in an effort to explain its causes and consequences. First, however, I cannot resist the temptation to pursue an analogy of the overextended debtor with the health-care field. We may regard the creditholic as afflicted by a debt disease. It is a chronic and not an episodic condition. Those who realize that they are helpless and dysfunctional will seek professional aid from credit counselors, the debt doctors. An appointment is made for a diagnostic conference. This initial session is often strained and tense. Like the psychiatrist who spends time developing rapport and trust, the credit counselor must be extra careful not to probe too intrusively. "People would rather reveal intimate details of their sex lives than their financial pickles," one credit counselor ruefully confesses.

After the malady has been carefully diagnosed, the credit counselor prescribes certain remedies—such as consolidation of debts, devising and maintaining a budget, stretching out loans, placing credit cards in limbo, suggestions for self-denial and for restraining impulse purchases, and living within one's means—until the debt disease is controlled and cured, hopefully within a certain time frame.

Part of the treatment may entail seminars or "group-therapy" sessions, such as Sacramento, California's "Spend-A-Holic" seminars in money management; or New York City's "Debtors Anonymous," a group modeled after the mutual self-help programs so brilliantly pioneered by Alcoholics Anonymous; or Westport, Connecticut's "Budget Advisory Service," which helps up-and-outers plan their finances systematically. Some of the "therapy" groups on debt management have devised ceremonial rituals, such as publicly cutting up credit cards and reciting litanies that confess weaknesses while requesting strength and wisdom.

Most people who realize that they have caught the debt disease and need help are not your ordinary deadbeats. They would like to pay their bills, but they have caught the contagion of overspending and excessive consumerism.

If all the remedial measures should fail and the debt disease spreads unchecked, then there is one final shock treatment to restore health—a declaration of personal bankruptcy. Bankruptcy is, indeed, shocking for some, but it is also a way of wiping clean the old slate, a means of being born again financially speaking. It is an action that is permitted once every six years. After bankruptcy has been filed, creditors may no longer hassle and harass the debtor for payment.

One further scene to draw from our analogy: A bankruptcy court is not unlike a mortuary where a funeral is being conducted. There is a quiet, even deadly, hush in the atmosphere. Participants in the proceedings speak in soft, subdued tones, seemingly not wishing to disturb or agitate the "dead." The lush, thick carpet in the court room is in maroon color. All the mourners are present and fighting back their tears. The attorneys and the trustees are dressed in funereal black, and the judge looks solemn in his or her black robe. The occasion is solemn and mercifully short, as the remains are parceled out to the various creditors. It is generally not a time for celebration and rejoicing. As with the morticians, the first people to get paid are the lawyers and trustees handling the bankruptcy case!

The only missing element from this procession of grief is the clergy. That work of consolation and bereavement comes as an aftermath of the bankruptcy proceedings. The sensitive pastor will mediate strength and sustenance in the subsequent hours of need.

Once the court has certified a debtor's insolvency, this event does not necessarily mean a full and permanent recovery. It is estimated that fully 61% of those who declare bankruptcy turn out to be recidivists. They catch the debt disease all over again after a short time. No sure-fire miracles exist for curing the afflictions of creditholism.

An increasing cause for alarm is the "deadbeat syndrone" that has come to characterize the American way of debt. What has become of the notion of the "sanctity of debt"? What does a promise to pay mean? So many people have defaulted that to the traditional warning, "Let the buyer beware," must be added the caveat, "Let the creditor beware!" There are those persons who run up large bills, knowing full well that there is no way they can possibly pay them. And there are those who borrow funds by signing a promissory note with full intention of disavowing their obligations when the debt payment falls due. Even a superior court judgment against such deadbeats is to no avail and only entails additional expenses to the creditor if the debtor so squanders funds or conceals assets that there remains nothing to collect. Only the lawyers, who often insist on suing, profit! A promissory note is only as sound as the party who signs it, and there seems to have emerged a class of pathological debtors who adopt the unprincipled attitude, "If you can get away with it, why not?"

In this respect, the experience of the federal government in collecting its debts has been an abject failure. At least $14 billion in outstanding debts remain uncollected. Senator James Sasser of Tennessee, chairperson of the appropriations subcommittee with jurisdiction in this area, reported that in 1978 losses due to bad debts amounted to $3.5 billion—an amount that had increased 60% in two years. Eventually, the thrifty, honest, hard-working taxpayers must pay off these debts in additional taxes.

Who are these delinquent debtors? The General Accounting Office reports that $1.2 billion is due in oil and gas royalties to the Interior Department. The Social Security Administration writes off debts as "hardship cases" with little or no investigation. One person with assets of more than $200,000 had a debt of $1,496 written off as "hardship." The Veterans Administration's educational aid loans were being written off as uncollectable even though the General Accounting Office found that many of these veterans had excellent credit ratings and sizeable assets and were owners of second homes.

Federal agencies have a policy of writing off debts of $600 or less on the grounds that collection efforts would cost more than the amount to be gained. As a result, countless persons pay off their debts down to the $600 level and then walk away from them, knowing full well that they will not be prosecuted.

Perhaps the widest publicity has been given to the student loans made through the U.S. Office of Education. The rate of default and delinquency of these loans is shockingly high and speaks volumes for the cavalier promises of America's educated class. Of the $4 billion loaned to students, fully $1 billion is in default. The likelihood that these debts for educational benefits will be repaid to the federal government is dim. Our sympathy would be evoked if most of these debtors could ill-afford to repay their student loans. Alas, such is not the case. Many have become prosperous and affluent individuals in the legal, medical, and dental professions. Ripping off Uncle Sam is simply a sport that hundreds of thousands of Americans are willing to play without furrowed foreheads or troubled consciences. Indeed, it is a game of one-upmanship.

It is not only the federal government that is victimized by the renunciation of legal and moral obligations to pay. In a classic line from Hamlet, Ophelia's wise father Polonius says to Laertes: "Neither a borrower nor a lender be; for loan oft loses both itself and friend." How true! Many have endured the painful experience of loaning funds to friends—only to have the friend renege on the loan and the friendship subsequently dissolved. Bosom buddies become bitter enemies over money-lending and defaulting. What is true of friends is equally true of relatives. Many siblings have intensified their rivalry over a renunciation of a promise to pay. Many families, once closely knit, have strained or broken relationships over loans. My remarks should not be interpreted as suggesting that loans ought never be made to friends or relatives. It may even be the case that the risk is worth taking and the price is worth paying. I am addressing myself to the deep disappointments and broken relationships occasioned by an unsuspecting and overly sanguine view in these matters.

It seems axiomatic to say that the easier the availability of credit, the greater the vulnerability to failures which lead to personal or corporate bankruptcy. More than 620 families in America each day declare bankruptcy. (By late summer of 1980, this figure had risen to 1,000.) Their acceptance of credit began as a blessing. But in bankruptcy their debts turn from dove to serpent and become a curse. Bankruptcy reflects the dark or shadow side of debt. It is the pathology of debt, the end result of the drunken use of credit. Unable to repay debts, strapped for funds, having put the applecart before the horse, the bankrupt person finds that not only has the applecart been upset, but he or she is buried beneath the pile of apples.

Approximately 85% of the bankruptcy cases in the nation are filed by individual consumers. No scarlet letter gives away the identity of the bankrupt person. He or she does not look any different or exude any peculiar odor to distinguish him or her from you and me. Bankrupt persons come from all walks of life. They are $100,000 corporate executives who work for one of the *Fortune* 500 firms, and they are unemployed welfare recipients. They occupy all income and education levels and come from all races and classes.

If one were to construct a profile of the "typical" consumer who has caught the debt disease, it might look something like this:

> —Head of a household of four persons
> —Mid-30s in age; man or woman
> —Gross annual income of $14,500
> —Debts averaging $7,500 due to 9 creditors
> —Spending roughly $400 per month more than is earned.

Business Bankruptcy

The debt disease is not simply an individual malady. Each year thousands of small businesses go under. At a time when countless couples are caught up in shifting gears or in a mid-course correction involving marriage and career crises, it may seem attractive and challenging to take a fling at starting one's own business.[30]

Take the case of a couple in their early forties who had become tired of climbing up the corporate wall. They took the plunge into starting a small distributorship of CB radios—at precisely the time when the CB craze had peaked and the bottom had fallen out of this over-inventoried and highly competitive market. Their venture failed miserably. Picking themselves up off the floor and screwing up their courage, they launched another business with their meager remaining funds, a second mortgage on their home, plus a generous loan from their bank. This time they entered the "can't-miss" faddish field of manufacturing shirts with embedded flashing lights for disco-dancers. The shirts were produced in abundance, but the lights malfunctioned. As misfortune would have it, they lost their own shirts and found themselves $125,000 in debt. Their only honest recourse: bankruptcy.

Of course, the odds against small enterprises succeeding are fairly high—perhaps at best a 50–50 chance when the economy is riding high. Things are never as easy as they appear to be in the first flush of planning when dreams are sky-high and hopes are projected with unbelievably profitable bottom-line numbers. In eight cases out of ten, the basic cause of business failure is managerial ineptness, incompetence, and inexperience. Other causes include insufficient staying power, undercapitalization, unanticipated operating expenses, poor location, rise in competition, high fixed costs, poor timing, slump in sales, neglect, and fraud.

As with individuals, so too businesses can abuse bankruptcy provisions. They can accumulate products and materials in abundance for which they pay no cash, then turn around and sell these goods quickly and either sequester the cash or claim they were robbed when they declare bankruptcy!

Not only small businesses must beware the bankruptcy trail, but also large companies may succumb. Less politically sensitive corporate giants than Lockheed or Penn Central may not have an uncle as munificent as Uncle Sam to bail them out. In February, 1979, the Chase Manhattan Mortgage and Realty Trust filed for bankruptcy. Its business was to loan money for real-estate development. It showed liabilities of more than $300 million and assets of only $270 million. Chase Manhattan Bank was the trust's advisor. If Chase can advise a trust that bears its name to declare bankruptcy, then small-business failures and individuals who default must consider themselves in good company. Corporations have the added advantage of being able to declare bankruptcy in a subsidiary without necessarily affecting the entire company.

Bankruptcy courts in the United States handle the largest volume of bankruptcy cases in the entire world. That is not a statistic of which we should be particularly proud. If America leads the world in bankruptcy proceedings, Los Angeles, California, has the dubious distinction of leading the nation. Through the portals of its Federal Court District pass an endless stream of debtors confronting creditors. In 1977, the L.A. district reported 19,704 filings—as many as the entire State of New York that year and more than the entire nation's quota in 1948. Not far behind Los Angeles in the hit parade of debtors going to bankruptcy proceedings is the District Court covering the San Francisco Bay area!

One can only speculate on why the experience of bankruptcy is more common in the United States generally, and in Los Angeles in particular, than anywhere else on the planet. Perhaps the freedom to succeed *and* to fail is greatest in America and in Los Angeles.

Although the frontier has long been closed, Los Angeles—that capital of cowboy movies and cowboy capitalism—still represents both symbolically and literally the spirit of individual enterprise. It is the home *par excellence* for those who dare and who risk in innovative ventures. The ghost of Horatio Alger particularly stalks the Southern California landscape. Many will try and some will succeed, but others flop.

Indeed, the West Coast is known for its innovative climate, for its inexhaustible energy that stimulates technological and commercial breakthroughs. It was possible for the Varian brothers and for Hewlett and Packard to begin their modest operations in backyard garages and flourish to become eminent industrialists and multi-millionaires, leading powerful, multinational corporations. Yet, as many succeed, countless others fail and beat a hasty path to the doors of the bankruptcy courts.

In the final analysis, bankruptcy is a mechanism for smoothing out the dislocations and tiding over the casualties or victims of our capitalistic system. Those who don't make it are given another chance to reenter the arena for yet another crack at the elusive prize. However cumbersome its legal provisions and proceedings, bankruptcy functions to facilitate our production and consumption economy. Instead of chaining people for years or for life to their debts, or stigmatizing them in a crippling fashion, bankruptcy is a humane method—when it is not abused —to encourage people and to keep them productive, to afford them hope for another day and another try.

For a presentation of the human drama of bankruptcy, we now turn to a concrete case history.

The Case of Paul Lazarus

Paul Lazarus (a fictitious name) became a well-known building contractor whose custom-made homes sold at a premium. His interest in constructing homes began in the late sixties after he remodeled his own Mill Valley, California, home and then sold it at a large profit. Amazed at the easy financial gain and growing bored by his work in computer parts sales, Paul, who had always been handy with the hammer, decided to enter the building business. He hired a contractor to build two houses on lots he had purchased in Fairfax. Working alongside the contractor as an apprentice, he soon learned the intricacies of the trade. These two houses were sold, again at a hefty profit.

His homes had a distinctive appearance, for he was very careful in his craftsmanship and took great pride in his work. Soon, home-buyers were coming to request his services. After building three more contract homes for individual parties, a real-estate agent came to him with an offer to sell nine acres of land in Corte Madera. He purchased the site and built 20 homes on it. Every one of these homes was sold prior to its completion. The Paul Lazarus Construction Company had built up a reputation for creating quality homes.

By now Paul had expanded his operation considerably. He rented office space and a shop for storing equipment, tools, paints, trucks, etc. His staff included a secretary, a bookkeeper,

16 carpenters, 2 painters, and 2 supervisors who worked out of the office. His work crews were busily building custom-designed homes as if there were no limits to demand. After all, he was operating in a highly desirable Marin County location. And he had no difficulty at all in securing credit from the bank for property purchases and construction loans. Indeed, the banker always greeted Paul with a broad smile and an extended, friendly handshake.

Overhead was high, but so were the potential profits. Within five years of Paul's going into the construction business, the radial saws were buzzing away at his job sites, which were scattered all over a growing Marin County. By now his firm was at work on 70 homes and his reputation as a young, reliable contractor was solid. Everything was going very well for Paul and his family, which included four children, ages 4 through 14. His lovely wife, Nancy, was busy buying furniture and decorating their beautiful new home, which Paul's firm had built in Tiburon. It had a breathtaking view of the San Francisco Bay.

By the spring of 1974, signs of trouble appeared. Home-buyers slowed to a trickle. Lenders tightened their loan policies, until eventually mortgage money seemed to dry up. The tight-money crunch was on, and the Paul Lazarus Construction Company was caught in its squeeze. Throughout that summer, houses simply were not selling. Paul had an inventory of $750,000 in unsold units. Meanwhile the bills were piling up. Payrolls had to be met. Interest charges were due to the bank. Payments to suppliers were being stretched out. Large sums were owed to the lumberyard and to various subcontractors for such things as plumbing, wiring, heating, flooring, concrete, and tile works. Now when Paul entered the bank, he was met with a scowl and questions about overdue payments.

Paul was plainly worried. Devoted to the church and active as a lay leader, he had always been a scrupulous person in handling money and in being fair in all his financial dealings. He thought to himself that there must be a way out of this tight predicament, that surely easier credit conditions would return in a few months. However, if any of his creditors were to attach a lien on his properties, such action would forestall any sales possibilities. Therefore, he decided to convene a meeting of his creditors. At the appointed time and place, Paul confronted 15 creditors who had retained the services of an attorney. Paul told them that he was having a hard time, that he needed their help, that in six years of dealing with them, he had never let them down. The group explored alternatives. Paul assured his creditors that he wanted to resolve the matter without resorting to bankruptcy.

The upshot of the meeting was that everyone agreed to cooperate and help out. Each creditor promised not to put a lien on the properties. An independent accountant would be hired at Paul's expense to reorganize the books and make payments to the creditors on a pro-rata basis. A committee of five of the largest creditors would oversee the rescue operation, and no checks could be written without being countersigned by one of the five. To show his good faith, Paul volunteered to add $50,000 of his remaining cash into a pool of funds under the management of the committee. The meeting ended on an upbeat, hopeful note.

After the session, Paul worked diligently to sell some of the houses. He reduced prices drastically and sought to interest buyers. It seemed that each buyer he brought into the bank was unqualified for mortgage funds. When the third prospective buyer did not qualify because he came $300.00 shy of the bank's formula for loans, Paul really blew up at the loan officer and demanded to speak to the branch manager. The manager politely assured Paul that the refusal was no reflection upon Paul, but that money was so tight that the head office in San Francisco simply would not approve, unless the loan was of the highest quality. He was sorry, but there was nothing that could be done. On his way out of the bank, Paul thought that the loan officer gave him a snide grin, as if to say, "See, I told you so." This so incensed Paul that he walked to the man's desk and tipped it over with a loud crash—to the surprise and shock of all the bank employees and customers!

After interminable meetings during the winter, the situation became more tense. One of the smaller creditors telephoned Paul in the evening, unleashed a steady stream of profanity over the wires, then threatened Paul with bodily harm. Not long after that incident, at one of the group's meetings, an elderly creditor, in a fit of irrationality, wanted to pick a fight with the much stronger and younger Paul. Finally, the plumber bolted from the group's plan and attached a lien on the property. Then it mushroomed. Other liens were attached, until it was useless even to show homes to prospective buyers.

Paul could not eat or sleep. He was deep in anguish and suffering in agony. He had nowhere to turn. He lost considerable weight, and his blood pressure rose dangerously. His own cash was depleted. He knew he was headed for either a mental or financial collapse—or both. He had that helpless feeling, like being trapped in a canyon with the flames licking at his feet. There was no escape route.

Finally, after much screaming and yelling at another one of his meetings with the creditors, Paul simply got up and walked out. A friend recommended that he confer with an attorney. Paul was told to face up to the reality that he was already in *de facto* bankruptcy, and he was referred to an attorney in San Francisco who specialized in bankruptcy cases.

In a brief session, the bankruptcy attorney, who himself was pressed for time (Paul claims his office was like an abortion mill), sized up the situation as follows: Paul was already beyond the provisions of Chapter 11, which enable reorganization and continued operation. He should file immediately for personal and corporate bankruptcy for himself and his spouse. He should homestead the house, protect his tools, and keep a car that is valued under $500. The lawyer recommended closing out bank accounts, converting cash into travellers checks and putting some cash in a concealed place.

Paul felt guilty about initiating all these proceedings, but the attorney reassured him that "The creditors are out to get you, so you've got to get them first." Also, Paul felt that he made a conscientious effort.

Shortly thereafter, Paul went to the regularly scheduled

weekly meeting with creditors and announced that he had filed for bankruptcy. If the hostility and anger had been high-spirited in previous meetings, it was now absolutely thunderous. Shouts, profanities, and curses were hurled at Paul. He barely escaped from the meeting with his hide intact.

Paul arranged for the deeds to the unsold houses to be turned over to the committee of five. Several years later, he inadvertently discovered that three of the major creditors bought off the others with fractional payments. In cooperation with the title company, these three creditors ended up holding title to the properties and later sold them at huge personal profits for themselves.

After the bankruptcy, Paul was thoroughly disillusioned. For a full year, he felt numb, shocked, and immobilized. He could do little else except walk around, as if in a daze, and read novels and brood.

In Paul's case, the crisis brought his entire family closer together. They supported one another, were quick to change their entire life style, learned to live simply with much less and enjoy it more. The Christmas of 1974 was particularly poignant, when the family gathered around the kitchen table, and Paul told the kids there would be no presents under the tree this year. In fact, there would be no tree. Paul felt so badly about this that he got up and went out for a walk around the neighborhood. By the time he returned home, the kids had topped off a fallen tree in the yard, dragged it into the house, set it up, cut out paper ornaments, and decorated it. What a sight when Paul returned! The family gathered around the "most beautiful Christmas tree" they had ever seen and sang "Silent Night." Tears of joy and gratitude were streaming down the cheeks of Paul and Nancy.

Nancy got a job working with children at a day-care center. The beautiful house in Tiburon was sold, and the family moved into a run-down, neglected old farmhouse near Petaluma. With his skills, Paul proceeded to remodel the old house into a very attractive and charming place. He had come full circle—back to the beginning point of remodelling an old house. His odyssey had taken him high to sniff the sweet smell of success, to live an affluent life style, to be a highly respected builder of specialty homes. The upward climb, though exhilerating, already contained seeds of discontent with shady business practices. The slippery slope of descent was absolutely horrendous, an experience so painful and humiliating that Paul would never want to endure those trials again.

What went wrong and why did a seemingly successful business venture fall apart so disastrously? There were many reasons, which, given five years of distance, Paul could now analyze perceptively. First of all, there were the financial circumstances of the economy, which Paul, as a neophyte contractor, had not previously experienced or prepared for. Suddenly the easy flow of funds contracted when the banks practically turned off the tap. Of course, they were acting in response to corporate decisions, which were made in response to federal banking directives. Paul admits that he was overconfident. He didn't seem to have reason for concern, because for the preceding three years, he could walk into the bank and practically write his own ticket.

Paul noted that he was highly leveraged, his expenses were top heavy, and his overhead and fixed costs were too high. Even though the product and the price were right, he simply grew too fast and lost control of the operations. He should have heeded the first warning signs and cut back on staff and building plans. Paul realizes that he made some poor judgments in trying to keep his work force together instead of tapering off. The homes he built are still avidly sought after, and prices have been bid way up; but five years ago, he was simply ahead of his time, overextended, stretched-out thinly, and vulnerable to collapse with a change of the credit tides.

We have seen in detail the rise and fall of Paul Lazarus. Today, Paul is a happy person living in a very congenial family setting in the countryside. To be sure, he has suffered; but he has also mellowed and matured. He has gained some chastened attitudes about human nature. Being a "nice-guy" type, he always felt that others were good-natured, well meaning, and above board. He is still disenchanted with the church, where, at one time, he mixed with his best friends. The minister was totally insensitive to Paul's crisis and completely wrapped up in his own ecclesiastical concerns. Instead of providing any support or consolation, the pastor even leaned on Paul for favors in doing free house repairs.

Years earlier, a couple in the church had fallen on difficult times. Paul and Nancy went to call on them. Before leaving their home, Paul left a $500 check on the dining room table and reassured his friends not to worry about repayment. The couple did get back on their feet and returned the $500 with grateful promises of reciprocal aid in the event of future need. However, when Paul and Nancy got into their own financial bind, this particular couple, as well as other old friends in the congregation, faded from sight. It was as if the Lazarus household had the plague and had to be quarantined.

Encouragement did come, however, from strange and unexpected places. Another couple in the church, whom Paul and Nancy had not known very well, wrote a note offering a loan of $1,000. That was a touching gesture.

Paul had been so disillusioned that he either sold or dumped most of his prized carpentry tools, assuming that he would never get back into the business. Out of the blue one day, a man for whom Paul had built a custom home five years earlier phoned and said, "I heard you went broke in the building business. I'm calling to ask you to build me another house." Paul replied that he was not interested, that he had had his fill of the business. The man insisted that they meet for lunch and talk things over.

Reluctantly, Paul went to lunch and heard words that snapped him out of his melancholy mood. The man said, "The best thing you could do is to take this job. It's like falling off a horse. You've got to get back on or else you will be crippled for life. I'm in no hurry; you don't even have to give me a price. Whatever you say, I know it will be right."

This kind of encouragement astonished Paul, who protested that he no longer even had the right tools. The man offered immediate cash to purchase the necessary equipment, plus a generous advance to get under way. Paul could hardly refuse such an offer. He felt affirmed as a human being. Paul assembled a makeshift crew and in just two months' work—which he called the "best therapy" in his life—built a fine house way below the price the man had been expecting to pay!

From that experience to this day, Paul has carefully limited himself to building one house a year with a select crew of young workers he takes great pride in training. He can control the entire operation, take a personal interest in each employee, and have ample time left over to pursue his hobbies, which include summer travel and photography. Nancy has continued her job, and the family is happier and more financially stable now than they ever were when they were living the hectic life high on the hog.

Paul realizes that if he had stayed in the competitive rat race of being a large contractor, he would have eventually eaten his heart out. The closeness he has with his wife and children now could never be purchased at any price. He thoroughly enjoys his work and its less frantic pace. No longer does total allegiance to the job dominate his entire life. No longer is Paul under any compulsion "to make it big."

If one could chart the stages, or the "natural history," of the evolution of Paul's experience from beginning to the present, the chart would show the following phases: (1) early exuberance with finding a new business that was interesting; (2) excitement with growth and development; (3) expansion and extension of the venture; (4) overextension or runaway operations that got out of control; (5) traumatic blow-up, hassles, and anger of creditors; (6) bankruptcy proceedings; (7) shock, immobility, limbo, disillusionment; (8) encouragement from friends or unexpected sources; (9) recovery of self-esteem; and (10) reconstitution of self and new work patterns.

Now we have viewed an entire case history of a real-life situation in which a conscientious but overly extended person fell victim to the trauma of bankruptcy. This is a story with a beginning, a miserable middle, and, fortunately, a happy ending. Not all bankruptcy cases end on such a pleasant note. Many are filled, however, with an equal amount of pathos and poignancy.

Several lessons can be learned from the case of Paul Lazarus. The first is to beware of borrowing funds in a reckless and indiscriminate fashion or without a prudent way of paying back. Being so highly leveraged and so thinly stretched out financially, Paul was obviously vulnerable and became the victim of changing monetary and loan policies. I have learned to become duly skeptical whenever I hear rave promises of great fortunes to be made in real-estate ventures by "tycoon"-type touters, who sell their programs and books to show people how to make a "killing" by using other people's money and no cash down of your own. Many people may succeed and be paraded as successful exhibits at public lectures, but be sure to confer with those who have failed.

Another clear lesson to learn from Paul's experience is that persons in bankruptcy need support, affirmation, and consolation. In many cases there is a deep sense of personal failure, inadequacy, and immobilization akin to Paul Lazarus's stunned feelings of psychological amputation. One wonders how long Paul might have remained in a dazed condition if an acquaintance had not unexpectedly reached out and insisted that Paul get back on the horse that had thrown him.

Aid may come from many sources—including family, relatives, friends—and even from surprising quarters. Bankruptcy is a time of pain and anguish, which many endure in silence and loneliness. It is a time when friends are particularly needed; yet mutual embarrassment often precludes friends from reaching out to each other. At the risk of becoming a "wounded healer," a friend can provide the encouragement that is supportive and sustaining.

A special source of assistance should come from the minister and the church fellowship. Instead of spurning or disassociating themselves from the bankrupt person, pastor and church members should be sensitive to the special needs and opportunities for ministry and caring during this period of personal financial distress. Otherwise, how are we to experience the meaningful reality of those frequently uttered words, "Forgive us our debts as we forgive our debtors"? Truly, there but for the grace of God go I.

Already the number of bankruptcy cases is alarmingly high. Millions of Americans are borrowing beyond their sensible limits. At these rates of indebtedness, even a moderate downturn in the economy will bring massive defaults and stepped-up activities by credit collection agencies. Creditors, in turn, may be hard pressed for cash if they are carrying heavy inventories and large accounts receivables. Both creditors and debtors are likely to feel the squeeze.

The personal dramas being enacted by the 600-plus families who declare bankruptcy every day in America must contain enough plots to fill a long-running television serial. In the early years of tv, a popular network series was called "The Millionaire." In fact, that series is currently being revived. Everyone wants to see or read about success stories. Who can bear hearing or seeing the sad tales about bankruptcy?

The ultimate ironic association of bankruptcy and the American way of debt is the link between debt and death. The American way of debt is even intertwined with the American way of death. In her hard-hitting book about the funeral industry, Jessica Mitford reminded us that not only are debts mourned, but mourners are debtors. Many American funerals are financed on credit. Death itself is paid for on time!

Our previous five chapters have reviewed various aspects of the debt disease and creditholism with its potential consequences for individuals and for the economy as a whole. We have documented the practice of excessive spending at all levels—from personal installment and credit-card purchases to persistently large national budget deficits. We have explored the connection between excessive credit and inflation. We have underscored the role of public faith and confidence in sustaining our debt-ridden economy in view of the straining of credulity when inflation exerts its toll.

Now we shall explore another facet of our problem, productivity. Some of the younger and newer voices among academic economists contend that the antidote to inflation is to increase personal savings as a source for capital formation for investment purposes and, also, to increase productivity. Both savings and productivity are at historically low levels, while inflation, debt, and consumer spending are exceedingly high. What is needed, therefore, are economic policies, enacted with political courage and leadership, to achieve a better balance between inflation and debt, on the one hand, and savings and productivity, on the other.

The rate of productivity—output per worker per hour—has been declining drastically in America. Many factors are responsible for this downhill slide, such as insufficient capital investment, research and development, new technology, and better management practices. One additional factor—frequently accorded lip-service in political rhetoric, but seldom probed for its significance—is the work ethic.

The next chapter explores the decline in worker productivity in relation to the erosion of the work ethic and the disenchantment with work. Positive suggestions are then sketched for the rehumanizing of work as a potential source for contributing to increased productivity.

VI
Whither the Work Ethic: Rehumanizing Work

One day, as a group of business leaders listened to a report on the state of the economy, the speaker suggested that the decline of worker productivity in America has meant that many of our products are inferior in quality and superior in price to goods being imported from abroad. A distinguished retired businessman at the meeting was shocked, dismayed, and surprised to hear this. "Why I thought American-made goods were superior to foreign products and always competitive in price," he countered. Try as he might, the speaker had a difficult time shaking the retired executive from his firmly held conviction.

It is nonetheless true that the Japanese and the Germans are able to produce more efficient and safer automobiles and have dragged Detroit kicking and screaming into the revolution of the small, fuel-efficient car. While Detroit simmered and protested, Volkswagon simply went ahead and developed a car that could travel 50 miles on a single gallon of gas.[31] In the television, steel, textile, and other industries, American productivity has fallen behind its foreign competitors. In some areas, American industry has become technologically obsolete and ineffi-

cient. Also, the growth in our economy that is fueled by debt
has far outstripped the growth that is based on production, so
that this enormous debt cannot be repaid from production at
stable prices.

From our discussion in the chapter on "Unlearned Lessons
from History," we have seen the tragic consequences of the
combination of inflation, a decline in productivity, and an increase in the supply of paper currency. Generally speaking, a
decline in productivity has inflationary consequences because
higher labor costs are not offset by increased output. As a result,
prices of goods and services climb.

ITEM: We have actually reached the point of decline in the
rate of productivity—or output per worker-hour—in
the private business sector. From 1947 to 1965, the
average rate of rise in productivity was 3.2% a year.
From 1965 to 1973, the average rise was 2.3%. Then
came a surprising and disturbing slide—to a bare 1%
rise per year from 1973 to 1978. And 1979 was even
worse, with an actual decline in the rate of productivity
to 0.1%.

The decline in productivity has focused a new searchlight on
the worker in America. For if productivity declines while inflation soars, we are surely headed for trouble. Many reasons have
been suggested for the stagnating productivity, which *Fortune*
magazine identifies as an even more disturbing sign of economic malfunction than inflation. Our discussion in this chapter, however, will be confined to the link between declining
productivity and the erosion of morale among workers as well
as the weakening of the traditional work ethic.

What has happened to the worker and to the work ethic that
has served so well to undergird the nation's industrial strength
and growth? This question is being raised with greater urgency,
given the instability of our economy and the lagging sense of
confidence.

Without doubt, there has been a transformation of the work
ethic. The spirit, enthusiasm, drive, and motivation seem to
have weakened, or, some would say, vanished entirely. A steady

stream of literature laments the fact that the work ethic in America is dead or dying. Observers characterize the situation by such descriptions as "disenchanted with work," "worker alienation," "work lacks fulfillment," and "work is boring and tedious."

Armed with tape recorder, author Studs Terkel traversed the nation, conducting verbatim interviews with workers from nearly all job classifications for his book *Working*. Terkel describes his research with this poignant comment: "This book, being about work, is, by its very nature, about violence—to the spirit as well as to the body. It is about ulcers as well as accidents, about shouting matches as well as fistfights, about nervous breakdowns as well as kicking the dog around. It is, above all (or beneath all), about daily humiliations. To survive the day is triumph enough for the walking wounded among the great many of us."[32] Whether it was corporate executive or secretary or truck driver or attorney or garbage collector, coal miner or waiter or mechanic, police officer or nurse or teacher or whatever, the net impression conveyed by Terkel's volume is a great sense of worker discontent and dissatisfaction. His reports of such low morale are all the more tragic in view of the author's conclusion that in three years of interviewing workers across the land, he never ceased to be amazed by the "extraordinary dreams of ordinary people."[33] Perhaps these workers were daydreaming, for surely they failed to realize their dreams on the job.

Terkel's perceptive analysis was based on what researchers would regard as "impressionistic" commentaries. However, any number of empirical studies, done under the rigors of sampling survey methods, would confirm Terkel's impressions. One of the latest studies (May 7, 1979) conducted by the Survey Research Center at the University of Michigan reports a sharp decline in worker satisfaction. Its index of job satisfaction, beginning with 100 in 1969, dropped to 98 in 1973, and then tumbled to 76 in 1977. The center reports that workers feel increasingly locked in to their present positions.

Like it or not, there is such a thing as the "white-collar woes" and the "blue-collar blues." Worker discontent is not just an exaggerated claim of soft-headed liberals. A federal grant to the Upjohn Institute to undertake a large-scale survey on a repeated or panel basis, first in 1971, then in 1973, came up with startling findings. In 1971, one-third of the workers sampled were dissatisfied with their jobs. The 1973 study of the same sample found job discontent much more pervasive. Upjohn's study concludes: "The job blahs are not confined to any work sector, but spread to every level and range of the work force. Now a majority of Americans—including white collar workers and executives—were dissatisfied with their jobs."[34]

Alas, work is one of those peculiar areas of life that is fraught with ambivalence. Many might claim that happiness in life is never having to work; yet, when not working, many people feel restless, useless, and lose their sense of worth and identity. Albert Camus has stated this ambivalence aptly: "Without work, all life goes rotten; but when work is soulless, life stifles and dies."[35] We may be disenchanted with our jobs, but we are even more dissatisfied when we are unemployed, or when we hear those shattering words, "You're fired!" We seem to be damned if we do and damned if we don't. This ambivalence has its roots in the biblical view of work, which we shall review shortly.

Another kind of ambivalence toward work has to do with what can be called the "underachievers" and the "overachievers." Allow me first to sketch a portrait of the underachievers. In the last decade a new generation has arisen which has adopted a more nonchalant, "can-take-it-or-leave-it-alone" attitude toward work. Instead of being compulsively driven by the need to work, to earn, and to save, this generation does not presume that work constitutes the major burden of life. In this view work is not the business of living, but simply a means to enable one to enjoy the art of living. With reference to the work ethic, I call those who adhere to this perspective the "underachievers." They are not necessarily lazy bums or cheaters. They simply feel that life is too important to be equated with working. They are content to work a few days or a few months, then take off to pursue their own interests. They would resonate with the sentiment expressed by the youth gang known as the Jets in *West Side Story* when they sang the lines: "We are not anti-social. We just don't like work." Underachievers would appreciate the office humorist's whimsical remark: "By working faithfully eight hours a day, you may eventually get to be a boss and work twelve hours a day."

Not being haunted by the ghost of the Great Depression, this new generation of underachievers feels the need to disengage from work periodically. Some are even in their forties and fifties and will "drop out" of their professions occasionally. Underachievers seem able to meet their basic needs and still live out some of their dreams—to travel, write, paint, play an instrument, photograph, hop on a freighter bound for distant lands, join a commune, or just be with intimate friends. When their funds run down, they will resume working, either full-time or part-time, until they can build up enough reserves to be independent from work again. Many underachievers are single, but some married couples adopt this life style as well.

Of course, there are those who abuse the free and casual life of the underachiever and do become free-loaders or welfare chiselers. Instead of earning their own keep, they prefer to be parasites upon society. Several years ago, a segment on the popular Sunday night tv series "60 Minutes" showed individuals who were living in Florida, playing golf and tennis or tending bar, assuming part-time jobs, while they were receiving monthly unemployment checks through the mail from Michigan, New York, and other northern states. Many viewers recoiled, their ire aroused, at this rip-off pattern being practiced with such skill and lack of a sense of impropriety.

By and large, however, the underachiever is ethical and simply wants the "space" to fulfill his or her own aspirations. At Lake Tahoe, California, I have met quite a number of fine, younger persons who live for the ski season and work on safety patrols during the winter. During the rest of the year, they assume part-time odd jobs as the need arises. They are solid specimens of humanity—clean-cut, good looking, athletic, sensitive, and articulate persons, who work hard when they are working. They simply are not driven by the compulsion of endless work. They are not hooked on the traditional work ethic. Some of them tell me they play tennis for Uncle Sam during the summer. When I ask if this means they are members of the Davis Cup Team, they reply, "No, it means I pick up my unemployment check, and then play tennis for a while!"

The life style of the underachiever may shock many who belong to an older generation born and bred on the work ethic of earning and saving all you can whenever you can. Yet, as a parent, I have learned to relax and not assume a judgmental, moralistic stance toward those who adopt this different pattern for living. It may not be my style, but, after all, America is traditionally regarded as the nation of pluralism or diversity; our's is a dynamic society that does not impose a cultural monism or monolith, but encourages freedom and diversity. This is part of the American dream and the American experiment, which is open-ended and ongoing. Once the experiment stops, the dream will likely turn into a nightmare.

Quite a different, but perhaps more familiar, orientation to work is what might be called the "overachievers." These workers have bought into the "achievement-success syndrone," which is one of the dominant value patterns of American society, so notes sociologist Robin Williams. To the overachiever, career goals are all-important. They strive many years, often at great financial cost and personal sacrifice to pursue their career objectives. They are familiar with deferred gratification.

The "good life" constitutes hard work, fierce dedication to the job, total commitment to the company. In time it will pay off handsomely in affluence and material rewards—a comfortable house with all the trimmings in Ross or Belvedere or Piedmont, California; Grosse Point, Michigan; Shaker Heights, Ohio; Edina, Minnesota; North Dallas, Texas; Lake Oswego, Oregon; or Darien, Connecticut.

The overachiever avidly reads Robert Townsend's best-selling *Up The Organization* in hopes of picking up tidbits for how to climb the organizational ladder, when, as a matter of fact, the

book is a spoof on the whole process, and its author has retired
to the warm waters of southern France, laughing all the way,
to enjoy the fruits of overachievement.

From the ranks of the overachievers come the "thrusters"
—those leaders with imaginative ideas, with the gift of charisma, who have stature and height, and determination to lead
and have others follow their command. They may be found
among the ranks of the entrepreneurs, in academic life, in the
ecclesiastical world, and in political and professional circles.
They are the people whose names are listed in *Who's Who in
America* and who are the toast of the town in society and gossip
columns. Their children "come out" for display at the debu-
tante balls.

The overachievers ride high in the saddle of society. Expect
them to be the patrons and sponsors of symphonies, ballet companies, and United Crusade drives. They generally receive the
plaudits and blandishments of the general public. They occupy
the command posts, for they know how to bear responsibility
with competence, charm, and grace. They are dependable, reliable, and trustworthy.

There is, on the other hand, a shadowy side that alienates
overachievers from their children, their spouses, and their
friends. Overachievers can be ruthlessly self-centered, overly
ambitious to serve their own ends, skilled in Machiavellian ma-
nipulation, highly competitive, always looking for new worlds
to conquer, polemical, and hard to live with! They are afflicted
with a disease that I have elsewhere dubbed "acute leisureitis,"
and which Wayne Oates more felicitiously calls "workaholism."[36]

Try as they may to disengage or to enjoy leisure, the overachiever is hooked on hard work and will experience withdrawal pains when on vacation, "after-work irritability," and
neuroses on weekends. He or she feels guilty when not busily
at work. He or she compulsively stuffs a daily briefcase full of
loose ends to tie up in the evenings at home. Always hard-
pressed for time, chained to a heavy, demanding schedule, the
workaholic has precious little time to spend with spouse, or

children, or close friends. Working is so associated with living that when work ends, life terminates too. The workaholic overachiever dares not release his or her tight grip on the brass rail of the merry-go-round of the workaday world that spins around and around like a dervish. To do so is to lose one's grip on life.

I have painted two contrasting portraits of ambivalent attitudes toward work in America. Each is an extreme type, perhaps even a caricature. Along the continuum between underachieving and overachieving, we can doubtless all identify ourselves.

Before probing for some of the reasons that lie behind the high level of worker discontent, I should like to return briefly to a discussion of the theological underpinnings of the work ethic—which in these days may be obscure. Since the Protestant Reformation, religous thinkers have developed quite an extensive body of literature to provide moral guidance or, some would say, to legitimize the work spirit in modern Western industrial civilization. This work ethic is a curious compound of Puritan and bourgeois values. Whether we are Protestants or not, we all live under its legacy. It is called the doctrine of vocation or calling.

In earlier centuries, the highest calling a person could conceivably fulfill was to serve God. That typically meant joining a religious order, becoming a cleric, going to a monastery or a convent, devoting oneself to a full-time religious task. Luther and Calvin, ushering in the Protestant Reformation, held the conviction that every person could serve God, not only in a religious calling, but also in the world and at the marketplace. The reformers taught the doctrine of "intra-worldly asceticism." The priesthood of all believers meant that the laity could also serve God as "ministers" in and through their jobs in the workaday world.

Indeed, work itself was viewed by the reformers as a holy pursuit. In *Religion and the Rise of Capitalism,* Richard Tawney quotes the early Swiss reformer Zwingli as saying: "Labor is a thing so good and Godlike that it makes the body hale and strong and cures the sickness produced by idleness. In the things of this life, the laborer is most like to God." Here we see a clear-cut connection between work and godliness. To see work as holy means that work brings with it a sense of wholeness, healthiness, a centeredness to life. Parenthetically, it is no accident that Calvin's Geneva and Zwingli's Zurich were to become banking centers, and that banking became a Protestant fine art and skill, a priestly calling in Switzerland.

In subsequent historical elaboration of the Puritan work ethic, such character traits and attributes as the following were important: thrift, hard work, industry, frugality, simplicity, diligence, discipline, sobriety, punctuality, self-reliance, and personal integrity.

Our New England ancestors believed that work is morally right, while idleness and play are sinful wastes of time. Recall that the Puritans arrived in the New World hungry, ill, homesick, and generally miserable. They faced the enormous task of carving out of the wilderness a new existence, and for the initial years that existence meant the struggle for survival. It was necessity that made them say, "The person who doesn't work doesn't eat." Far from being prudish or fanatics, the early Puritans were intelligent, dedicated persons who sought to live useful and responsible lives under the sovereignty of God and the authority of the Scriptures. Only six years after the colony led by John Winthrop arrived, they founded a little institution known as Harvard College!

A useful and responsible life was rooted in work. That meant that through work the Christian made a useful and responsible response to God. As Richard Steele wrote in *The Tradesman's Calling,* published in 1684: "God doth call every man and woman . . . to serve him in some peculiar employment in this world, both for their own and the common good. . . . The Great Governour of the world hath appointed to every man his proper post and province, and let him be never so active out of his sphere, he will be at a great loss, if he do not keep his own vineyard and mind his own business."[37] For the Puritan, then, the choosing of a vocation meant trying to discern what work

God was calling him or her to do. Work was also exalted as a defense against wasting time. As one account has it, the New England Puritans drank a pint of yeast before going to bed at night to make them rise early in the morning for work.

Such a responsible view of work, together with its fruits of thrift, frugality, and the rest, could not help but lead eventually to economic success—a fact which has led Max Weber and Richard Tawney to their conclusions about Puritan ethics and the rise of capitalism.

Now the reformers were not alone in their lofty assessment of work. At the very beginning of the Bible, in the Book of Genesis, God or Yahweh is depicted as the Cosmic Worker. God labored diligently to fashion the Creation. God even enjoyed the Creation and, while resting on the seventh day, assessed it as a very good piece of work. Here is certainly a lofty view of work. To be identified with work, then, is to be a co-creator with God, to share in the joy of creation. Work is glorified, and the worker is dignified.

Very early in the biblical account, however, there is expressed another shadowy or ambivalent side of work—its association with pain, travail, toil. In this view, work was seen as punishment, as a curse, as necessary suffering, as banishment from the Garden of Eden. This eviction notice by the Heavenly Landlord to Adam and Eve meant that they had to get out and earn bread by the sweat of their brows. Human beings were consigned to toil on the soil, from whence they came. In effect, through work human noses were rubbed in the dirt and soil of existence.

I believe it is important to capture a sense of the ambivalent character of the biblical understanding of work, lest we see work only in its grandeur and not in its misery. Surely we have traveled a long distance away from the sense of the holiness of work. Few Americans share the Reformation-era perception that what they are doing on the job is akin to godliness or is God-like, despite a well-articulated doctrine of vocation preached from hundreds of thousands of pulpits. As for the other biblical view of work—as toil and suffering—if work is such a burden and a curse, what modern-day American, accustomed to the comforts of life and unwilling to endure oppression of any sort, would want anything to do with it? In either case, there is a waning of the work ethic.

Our secularized, desacralized world has unhinged itself from the obligation of working to please God or to discover God's laws in the universe and in nature. It is quite possible that a deeper source of the renunciation of work is to be found in the shedding of religious convictions about the meaning of life, the stewardship of time, and the primacy of faith. After all, if life has little meaning, if it is filled with the sense of absurdity or terror, if history has no providential purpose, then why bother? What's the use? Why knock ourselves out working? Work can't be all that important. Why not simply enjoy our hot tubs and be stroked by peacock feathers?

In addition to this fundamental theological explanation for turning our backs on the work ethic, what other reasons should we consider? Without exhausting the possibilities, I want to mention four more factors: (1) Work is a grind. (2) Work is dehumanizing and demeaning. (3) Work is a competitive rat race. (3) Work is fragmented.

Work is a grind. Perhaps the most common gripe workers have about their jobs is the monotony and tedium involved. Routine operations and repetitive patterns have robbed work of a sense of newness, excitement, or adventure. Doing the old familiar tasks over and over again only heightens the sense of boredom and encourages the worker to long for an escape hatch, to try something new and different.

Monotony and boredom are not feelings confined simply to menial jobs or assembly-line operations. Similar sentiments are shared by lawyers, church leaders, professors, and others who feel stale and trapped into old grooves that are well worn. In an ungracious reference to an older colleague, one young instructor remarked, "Professor X has not been teaching for thirty years; he has taught one year thirty times!"

Boredom, of course, is a disease of the soul. It gnaws away at the innards and creates an inner impoverishment of the restless spirit, until a mood of apathy, disinterest, and aimlessness prevails. Time on the job is spent watching the clock, counting the hours and the minutes, being "distracted from distraction by distraction."

To press home the point that for many people work has become a grind, I want to relate the experience of a middle-aged, nice, but not particularly attractive, woman, who, half-shocked and half-amused, told me this story. Her dentist is a kindly, older man to whom she had been going for more than 15 years. One day, while she was sitting in his dental chair, with her mouth wide open and eyes closed, anticipating the dreaded drill bit, the dentist suddenly planted a kiss smack on her open mouth! Now, she asked in disbelief, why on earth would he do a thing like that? My reply: That's simple, his job is a *grind,* and he merely wanted to break the monotony!

One rather transparent means of overcoming the tedium is to confer dignified and euphemistic titles. Thus the janitor is the "sanitation engineer," the stock broker is the "account executive," the Kodak salesperson is the "branch account specialist," the grave digger is the "caretaker," the gardener is the "superintendent of grounds," women in service jobs are called "pink-collar employees," and the number of "vice presidents" in a large bank is greater than Carter has pills.

Work is dehumanizing and demeaning. Another frequent complaint about work is its degrading and dehumanizing character, wherein the worker is made to feel like an IBM card, a payroll number, or a mechanical robot. You shall be known by your digits! Office workers or secretaries who assume quasi-executive responsibilities are often placed on a tracking system. Once they reach the top of their scale, there is no further room for mobility. Thus, they feel they are not being treated like persons, not being fully appreciated for their contributions, but are regarded as slots in a system, as faceless interchangeable parts which are expendable.

Frequently the assembly line worker feels less than human. There is a psychic strain that makes it difficult, if not impossible, to keep up with a task that relentlessly comes on stream—unless the person assumes the same characteristics which the machine possesses. As a form of protest, automobile workers on the Detroit assembly line are known to respond in several ways: wildcat strikes over the pace of the line, high rates of absenteeism, sabotaging the process by throwing a monkey wrench into the machinery and requiring a shut-down or rest period, and letting a car go by without performing the assigned function. This car then comes to the consumer as the dreaded "lemon."

Stories about assembly-line behavior are legendary. I shall resist temptation and only relate one of them. A certain automobile owner kept hearing a rattle in his brand new Chrysler. Try as he might to discover the source of the irritation, success eluded him. In desperation, he took the car into a shop. There the lining on his back door was ripped open, revealing a whiskey bottle with a note inside. The message read: "Bet you had a helluva time finding this one." This admittedly adolescent behavior is a symbolic means of expressing the worker's humanity. It shouts out, in effect, "I am a human being, not a nobody or a machine!"

Work is a competitive rat race. Worker discontent leading to the temptation to "drop out" or to change jobs is often attributed to the fact that working has become a competitive rat race. Workers, like rats, are caught up in the maze and competing fiercely among themselves for the scarce goods, privileges, promotions, and positions. Certain behavioral codes that exert pressure toward conformity and rob the person of individuality and freedom become intolerable.

Corporate bureaucracies require people to follow orders. Work is so organized as to minimize independence of the worker and maximize control and predictability by the organization. Activity is geared to a high production schedule, and profit growth must exceed previous comparable periods. Or sales quotas are set and revised upward, so that one must run just to stay even, not to speak of trying to get ahead. The pace that is set by the machine or the machine-like manager, the relentless drive for efficiency, the hassle of supervisors to follow their orders to a "t," the competitive spirit that is behind the race to get ahead—all these things create worker resentment and a longing to leave the rat race before one's sanity is lost.

Many middle managers feel compelled to compete in order to gain the attention of top management for support of projects or for promotions. This competition leads to tension, conflict, and frustrating in-fighting.

Being fed up with the rat race, the worker may spill over his or her job-generated frustrations into aggressive behavior toward family, neighbors, friends, or the helpless cat that happens to be in the way. Or fatigue, mental anguish, psychic sores from the day's labor may create a sullen, unresponsive, sexually impotent, moody person, who goes home, collapses, and stays glued to the television all evening.

Willie Loman, as depicted in *Death of a Salesman* by Arthur Miller, is perhaps the most memorable tragic-hero figure in American literature. Willie is a victim of the dog-eat-dog competitive sales world. He simply could not keep up with the younger competition that displaced him. At his grave site, his disillusioned son Biff sadly says, "Poor Willie, he didn't know who he was."

Increasingly, workers who feel trapped or caught up in the competitive rat race have decided to quit, take on a new vocation, or return to a professional or trade school for retraining.

Work is fragmented. The loss of meaning in work, the absence of a sense of wholeness or fulfillment is frequently attributed to the segmented or fragmented nature of many jobs. One participates in a small piece of the operation with no sense of the finished product, of craftsmanship, of completion. Fragmentation of work engenders segmental participation or only partial involvement of oneself in the task.

Workers who perform specific and limited functions often feel locked in to their jobs. They may lack the skills for advancement. They may feel they are trapped in a "dead-end job." However, it is not simply unskilled recent immigrants or racial and ethnic minorities who harbor these feelings. Highly trained technical specialists may also suffer from fragmentation. This is what the best-selling book *Zen and the Art of Motorcycle Main-*

tenance is getting at—if I understand it at all! Harvard social scientist, David Reisman points to the narrow, technical training in our educational system that produces dissatisfied specialists in later career pursuits.

One of the consequences of work fragmentation is the sense of alienation. Robert Blauner identifies four ingredients of worker alienation: powerlessness—regarding ownership, general management policies, employment conditions, and the work process; meaninglessness—with respect to the character of the product worked on, scope of the product, or the production process; isolation—lack of relationship to the social aspects of work; and self-estrangement—depersonalized detachment, including boredom, leading to the absence of personal growth.[38]

If Willie Loman is symbolic of the inability to cope in a competitive climate of sales, then television's comic-tragic figure Archie Bunker epitomizes the forgotten American breadwinner who is alienated from society and distrustful of youth, racial minorities, and people unlike himself, always harboring a sense of personal and political inadequacy.

Doubtless the four reasons we have cited do not exhaust the explanations for worker discontent. However, they do provide clues for understanding the decline in productivity in the American work force. In recent years, a movement has emerged to counter some of the negative consequences of worker dissatisfaction. I call this the "rehumanization-of-work movement." A thoroughgoing treatment of this trend is beyond our immediate scope; however, it may be instructive to point out some of the positive directions that are being taken to improve worker morale and meaning on the job— especially since these issues relate to the problem of declining productivity in America. Here, briefly, are some promising developments.

Share in Decision-Making and Profits. The call to redesign work and to rehumanize the work place gives high priority to enabling the worker to have a share in decision-making processes and to have a piece of the action, or to participate in profit sharing through bonuses or incentive systems. Note that in Japan it is customary for workers to receive an end-of-the-year bonus equivalent to three or four months of an employee's salary. When Americans see Japanese tourists by the bus loads, they may be sure that these travelers are enjoying their bonuses.

Worker participation in making decisions assumes many different forms, from informal to formal arrangements and from conversations to the process of matrix management, which draws persons from different work sectors to focus on particular tasks.

As for profit sharing, one plan now being adopted is known as ESOP (Employee Stock Ownership Plan). Its originator is a San Francisco attorney, Louis Kelso, author of *The Capitalist Manifesto.* Kelso's plan, which has captured widespread attention, would allocate company shares to workers based on certain criteria, so that over the course of time the employees would become owners. The ESOP and its variations obviously stimulate workers to take a greater interest in their jobs and motivate them to work for the success of the firm, because their own self-interest is involved.

Career Planning and Retraining. Since much job dissatisfaction entails being in the wrong place at the wrong time with the wrong people, or else shifts in interest and enthusiasm, larger companies increasingly have personnel officers who counsel employees on their career plans. If necessary, job shifts are made within the organization or to another location or with another company. Actually much could be learned about the shortcomings of an organization if its top officer were to counsel with those who have resigned. Entrance interviews are common, but exit ones are rare.

It is said that a typical worker changes jobs about seven times over the course of a career. Planning and retraining aid will help smooth the transition process of shifting gears. It is better for the person and for the organization to have a contented worker than a disgruntled one. In Berkeley, California, an organization known as Work/Net engages in job counseling, referrals, workshops and seminars for career planning, guidance, and retooling.

Sabbatical Leave Plans. Traditionally a privilege granted in academic circles after six years of teaching, the sabbatical leave is increasingly being adopted in management ranks. Xerox and General Electric, for example, have extensive programs for their executives to take sabbatical service leaves with full pay. Actually sabbaticals are too good a thing to be confined to the groves of academe. Some of the nation's best talent and resources are in the corporate ranks, and sabbaticals release the talents of executives to serve as aides in projects that benefit the community at large. The worker returns to the job refreshed, with a new perspective, and the company can take pride in knowing that it has contributed something to the community's well being.

Job Enrichment Programs. Any number of firms, such as General Electric, General Motors, Ford, and IBM, sponsor programs for job enrichment. These programs include such things as special seminars, lectures, films, discussion groups, and educational tours—usually subsidized wholly or in part. Some companies even underwrite advance study for academic degrees for their employees, and universities have responded with tailor-made programs. The University of San Francisco Extension has many such offerings. The San Francisco Theological Seminary's degree program in the Master of Arts in Human Values is currently in discussion with corporations to contract for study programs at corporate sites.

Management Style: Shift from Theory X to Theory Y. Corporate leadership patterns of "collegial management" are increasingly replacing the traditional hierarchical management styles. There is a management shift from Theory X to Theory Y. These twin theories are associated with the name of Douglas McGregor, professor of management at MIT, who died in 1964, and they are based on different assumptions about human nature.

Theory X assumes the following:

- Management is responsible for organizing the elements of productive enterprise—money, materials, equipment, people—in the interest of economic ends.

- With respect to people, this is a process of directing their efforts, motivating them, controlling their actions, and modifying their behavior to fit the needs of the organization.
- Without this active intervention by management, people would be passive, even resistant, to organizational needs.
- The average person is by nature indolent, that is, he or she works as little as possible.
- He or she lacks ambition, dislikes responsibility, prefers to be led.
- He or she is inherently self-centered, indifferent to organizational needs.
- He or she is by nature resistant to change.
- He or she is gullible, not very bright, the ready dupe of the charlatan and the demagogue.

On the other hand, McGregor's Theory Y follows another set of assumptions:

- People are not by nature passive or resistant to organizational needs. They have become so as a result of experience in organizations.
- The motivation, potential for development, capacity for assuming responsibility, the readiness to direct behavior toward organizational goals are all present in people. Management does not put them there. It is a responsibility of management to make it possible for people to recognize and develop these human characteristics for themselves.
- The essential task of management is to arrange organizational conditions and methods of operation so that people can achieve their own goals best by directing their own efforts toward organizational objectives.
- Human growth is self-generated and furthered by an environment of trust, communication, and authentic human relationships.[39]

The emphasis in Theory Y is on open communications and relating to workers as human beings with potential to fulfill. McGregor's book is still widely read, and there has been recent controversy about whether or not Theory Y expectations impose too great a strain on certain work situations. Nevertheless, the shift from the Theory X– to the Theory Y–style of management leadership is in line with efforts toward rehumanization of the work place.

Safe Work Place. Tragic accidents due to unsafe or hazardous work conditions also contribute to worker discontent. Deaths from industrial accidents are still rather commonplace. In fact, if we take the year 1968, because the Vietnam War was still raging, there were more deaths from industrial accidents that year (14,311) than there were American soldiers killed on the Vietnam battlegrounds. In addition to health hazards at the job site, companies must be sensitive to their effluence, their industrial pollutants, the lung and cancer diseases of an asbestos plant, for example, whose dust is carried by the wind and settles in a community 25 miles away.

I was shocked and dismayed to hear from a post-office official that one cent out of each 15¢ postage stamp goes to pay off worker compensation for job-related injuries. Since a considerable amount of heavy lifting of packages and sacks of mail goes with the job, back injuries are frequently reported. Such injuries entitle the worker to 45 days off for recovery. One postal employee, having claimed back injury, was photographed leaping over the net to receive his tennis trophy, which he won in a tournament during his period of recuperation!

Well-Time Leave. We are all familiar with sick leave—which sometimes is taken whether a person is sick or not. Libby Owens Ford has successfully experimented with "well leave" or time off for being well. Amazing how this cuts down on absenteeism due to "illness." If a worker has a perfect no-sickness record for one year, an additional week's vacation is granted. This program of positive reinforcement does wonders for the health of the American worker!

Flexitime. This innovation enables the worker to devise a schedule to suit his or her own needs and responsibilities. A worker is entitled to design an eight-hour work schedule that enables better commuting patterns. There is less fatigue and less time wasted going to and returning from work during the commuter rush hours when the roads or public transportation facilities are jam-packed. A Scott Paper Company employee who has adopted a 7:30 a.m. to 3:30 p.m. work schedule reports that this arrangement gives her more time to spend with her family, especially during the after-school hours when her children come home. She notes that flexitime has boosted her morale and her productivity at work. Besides, she can prepare a better meal for her hungry husband when he arrives! Working mothers particularly are grateful for flexitime.

New Work Patterns. We are still at the early stages of trying out new styles of work that can create more fulfillment and job satisfaction. One such possibility is job sharing, whereby a single position may be voluntarily shared by several workers, none of whom wishes to work a full day. This is already possible at Standard Oil of California. Another pattern is shorter working hours or part-time employment. Some companies encourage a program of staggered retirement or tapering off toward the end of one's career. The future may well see more couples working together. We are seeing this already in the ministry. Since half of our students preparing for the ministry are now women, ordained clergy couples are increasingly seeking joint appointments as church leaders.

Grievance machinery for settling disputes and for resolving conflicts—whether in the form of an ombudsman or a representative committee of one's peers—is still another feature of the humanization process. Fireside chats or coffee hours with free interchange and dialogue between top management officials and other employees have been adopted by some firms.

Freedom from Seduction. Although not a new problem, sexual harrassment has increased along with the increase in the number of women in the work force in nearly all occupations —from police patrol to military life to forestry service, in addition to hospitals and sports writers interviewing in men's locker rooms. Many women find themselves being coyly seduced while seeking employment. There is growing resentment among women in the work force who are particularly offended by the necessity of fending off sexual advances. Repeated suggestions made implicitly or explicitly concerning rewards or punishment for sexual favors are being viewed indignantly. The question of women's concerns about sexual coercion has brought to the work place awareness groups and assertiveness training as well as rape-prevention classes to prepare women better to cope with overly aggressive men.

Consultation and Study Centers. Continuing research and consultation services are provided by a number of academic centers. At UCLA, for example, a "Center for Quality of Working Life" confers with management and labor to redesign the job situation with humanization in mind. Some of the center's proposals call into question conventional practices and procedures. A few examples: (1) Break up the assembly line into smaller working units to give a sense of control and promote employee participation in making decisions, thereby overcoming the problem of fragmentation. (2) Eliminate invidious signs of privilege and elitism—such as reserved parking spaces, thick carpets, private jets, company cars for personal use, executive dining rooms, private toilets and showers, and membership at exclusive clubs. (3) Encourage work pride, self-initiative, quality work, and productivity.

I have listed various signs of the efforts currently under way to stem the tide of worker disenchantment. Whether these endeavors merely deal with the surface symptoms or affect basic causes is difficult to say. The connection between low morale and absenteeism among workers is clearly established by industry studies. It is also true that the cost of absenteeism amounts to an annual tab of $30 billion. That amount in loss productivity is significant. That amount is also equal to the entire national budget deficit projected for the year 1980!

The work ethic may be dormant or dying or even dead, and our paradoxical and ambivalent attitudes toward work may remain unresolved. If so, American productivity seems destined to fall further and further behind the output of other nations. Various measures directed at the rehumanizing of work may help, at least partially, to stem the tide of worker disenchantment and declining productivity. Coupled with unchecked inflation and the ever-growing supply of paper currency, declining productivity provides ample grounds for concern about the prospects of the American economy in the period just ahead.

It is well to remind ourselves that no simple or magical formulas or recourse to gimmicky techniques should be expected in the search for solutions to problems so deep-seated and brewing for so many decades. Indeed, my conviction is that the road to finding answers is best sought in a clarification and change of perspectives, rather than in developing specific blueprints, which are likely to be premature. Hence, the final chapter is a dialogical response to the issues of excessive credit, inflation, and the prospects of economic collapse from the perspective of faith, social ethics, and confidence.

VII
Econ-fidence:
Faith and Economics

"Faith seeking understanding" is a commonly accepted definition of theology. To underscore the ethical thrust, I prefer to say, "faith seeking understanding through love and justice." Theology and ethics are two sides of the same coin. Christian social ethics is sometimes viewed as "doing the truth" (to emphasize its action component) or as probing the presuppositions upon which human decisions are based (to accent its critical reflection task).

Social ethics is a dialogical discipline that relates theology to the various cultural studies, including economics. In this dialogue, there is ample room for interplay. For example, one of theology's concerns is with grace—the grace of God, which is in abundant supply, is freely given with no strings attached, and with no regard for merit. Economics, however, deals with scarcity, with a limited supply of resources, money, and personnel. Economics must wrestle with problems of allocation of limited commodities, whereas grace knows no limits. When these two perspectives collide, it makes for dialogue that is not always compatible.

Our preceding chapters have argued that *fides*, or faith, is the link that sustains the economy. Faith may be viewed in many ways—as allegiance to certain beliefs or affirmations about God, such as embodied in the Apostles' Creed; as a historical religion, such as the Christian or the Buddhist faith; as a profound religious experience of the presence of Christ in one's life. Still another dimension of the meaning of faith—with particular relevance to a societal context—refers to the sense of a relationship of mutual trust and fidelity between persons, and in corporate or societal interactions.

Two outstanding theological ethicists, James Gustafson and the late H. Richard Niebuhr, have explored this dimension of faith as confidence and trust, loyalty and fidelity.[40] To have faith is to trust, particularly as one enters into a relationship of economic exchange. Certain obligations and mutual expectations are required in a relationship of faith.

In a very real sense, our economy lives by faith, lives in the confidence that other persons and social institutions are reliable and trustworthy in their dealings. The absence of faith, loyalty, and fidelity breeds suspicion, fear, and distrust. When faith is broken or confidence is shattered, the seeds are sown for social chaos and economic disorder. Faith is such an important prerequisite for a viable economy that I have coined the term "econ-fidence" to reflect the interrelatedness between economics and confidence. Without public faith or confidence, our money system would collapse.

Faith Seeks Honesty

At its root, the problem facing our economy is a breakdown in confidence, which, if unchecked, could lead to fear and panic. Credibility is an elusive quality, an intuitive feeling that cannot be wholly confined within rational bounds. Confidence is difficult to build up, for its foundation stone is trust and rapport. If *fides*, or faith, is removed from the word confidence, we are left with "con" which means "with" or "together." In our context, it could also mean being conned or deceived or duped.

Public delusions and crowd hysteria are volatile and unpredictable, once the chain of *fides* is broken. Deep-seated and dormant emotions of fear are unleashed and seem to run through their inexorable course before confidence can be restored—much as a fever must spend itself before health is regained.

At first I suspected that the Proposition 13 movement in California was one of those irrational public responses. I dismissed it as merely taxpayers' greed reasserting its own selfish interests. Now I see its larger symbolic significance. The public revolt of taxpayers, spreading nationwide in the wake of California's Proposition 13 experience, is an important mythic symbol of our time. Indeed, it is to the older generation what Woodstock was for youth. A cultural myth—in our context—is no fairy tale for the pacification of childlike minds. Rather, a myth is a profound sign or happening with a certain ineffable character, an action thrust which metaphorically captures a reality, the full meaning of which is elusive and cannot be exhausted by ordinary categories of speech alone.

Proposition 13 is a mythic message, a warning, that for too long the absurdities of the system have gone unchallenged. Waste, excessive spending, profligacy are not to be tolerated. The reaction of Proposition 13 is not just taking offense at too many taxes being levied, but the desire to place a check on the practice of the irresponsible spending of other people's money —funds that would not be so recklessly spent if they were one's own. The moral is: "Spend other people's money as you would spend your own." Mythically interpreted, Proposition 13 is a testimony to the fact that for too long the dialogue on economic issues has been confined to the economic "generals" and government officials. Proposition 13 is saying, in effect, the public wants to participate, wants to break up this incestuous discussion that has establishment economists and politicians locked in mutual embrace. Their conversation has produced a well-grooved, worn-out record of tinkering, tampering, and tuning —when the public knows that fine (or even gross) tuning is no longer operative. What is called for is a fundamental realignment of priorities. Nothing short of a transvaluation of values or a moral revolution will suffice. Faith requires no less than honesty.

The mythic significance of Proposition 13 is greater than its proponents could possibly have envisioned. I am certainly no admirer of Howard Jarvis and the real-estate interests he represents. I am more attracted to the plea of a Solzhenitsyn, whose plain and candid charge to the Western capitalist nations is surely a rebuke. This exiled prophet rejects the moral debasement of uncontrolled materialism. He resurrects the age-old contest between materialism and spirituality. Mammonism has gained the high ground at the moment. Solzhenitsyn is not alone on this score. Note that Pope John Paul II's first encyclical condemns consumerism because it exalts materialism at the expense of the spirit and makes human beings the slaves of things. Both Solzhenitsyn and John Paul call for a revolution of the spirit. Their pleas naturally fall on shocked hearers or deaf ears in a nation of spenders who are hooked on the acquisition of material things.

Would that we could express the same sense of confidence, nonchalence, and spiritual freedom that permits us to join with the disciple in Christ who said, as I paraphrase it: "I have learned to manage on whatever I have. I know how to be poor, and I know how to be rich, too. I have been through my initiation, and now I am ready for anything anywhere; full stomach or empty stomach, poverty or plenty." (Phil. 4:11–13).

The drift toward materialism has turned into a menacing tide. Fleshed with Solzhenitsyn's substance, Proposition 13's larger significance is reminiscent of the parable told by Søren Kierkegaard about the clowns. A group of clowns had been traveling across the prairie when they spotted a raging fire sweeping its way toward the town. They rushed into the village square, with costumes still on, and began warning the people that "A fire is coming! A fire is coming! Prepare for it!" Having in mind the opening of the circus the next day, the people could scarcely control their laughter. "Aren't these clowns funny;

why of course we'll be coming to the circus." Disaster struck, as the clowns had predicted, and the town was destroyed. Comedy turned into tragedy.

A warning has been sounded. The California vote has been heard around the country. The people refuse to keep silent. They are ready to storm the citadel of the nation's capital if that's what it takes to enter into the dialogue between economists and policy-makers. The people will not be fooled or deceived or denied forever.

ITEM: Any number of eminent economists, such as Milton Friedman, Paul Samuelson, and Walter Hoadley, would concur with James S. Dusenberry's assessment of gold. Writing in a standard textbook, after Nixon had closed the gold window, Dusenberry claimed that the dollar imparts value to gold, rather than gold imparting value to paper dollars.[41] He asks rhetorically: "What would happen to the value of gold if the U.S. Treasury refused to give $35 for each ounce of gold offered to it? It is clear to everyone what has happened: The dollar has declined in value, whereas gold has zoomed ahead from $35 to nearly $900 until the price began to fluctuate wildly.

Small wonder the average person in the street begins to suspect such incongruity between theory and practice and loses confidence in the wisdom of expert economists who advise the federal government on its policies.

Faith demands no less than a policy of honesty in dealing with public issues. The public sincerely wishes to have a sense of confidence in its political policy-makers. After all, they are the "best and the brightest." If, however, the public begins to suspect that some sort of cruel hoax or deception is being perpetrated, then the confidence factor could decline precipitously.

ITEM: Through inflation, there is a steady and inexorable increase in the real rate of taxation, as taxpayers are pushed into higher tax brackets. Is this a deliberate policy to raise federal spending levels?

If confidence is to be restored, the government and the policy-makers must work "with" the people and not try to "con" them. It is interesting to note the emergence of a new breed of younger economists who share the democratic conviction that intelligence is spread out among the people and not concentrated in Washington, D.C. One representative of what is known as the "rational expectations" school, Robert Lucas, points out that "consumers have been deceived and businessmen have been tricked by inflation: We think people are as smart as we are. . . . They don't have to be brilliant or study the latest figures from the Fed to know about inflation and the effect of Government spending." Lucas continues, "You can't run a democratic society by trickery. Since people aren't stupid, mere declarations of Government intentions are just about meaningless. To talk about reductions in taxes is meaningless if such measures are not accompanied by a decrease in Government spending."[42] Although the consideration of rational expectations in the plans people make is thus far a modest contribution of this economic school, the spirit of the new breed is commendable—for faith seeks humility and honesty where public policy is concerned.

Faith Seeks Community:
The Shift from Ego-Ethics to Eco-Ethics

An impressive outpouring of literature predicting gloom and doom has appeared in recent years. Rough times are ahead, warns Howard J. Ruff. Depression, dictatorship, and brown-outs are future prospects, predicts Harry Browne. It should come as no surprise that the most solid and serious work in the recent spate of dyspeptic literature Robert Heilbroner's *The Human Prospect* has not met with the same kind of commercial success as the Ruff and Browne writings.

There is certain merit and cogency to the arguments being advanced by these bad-news bearers. I share many of their concerns as to the fragility of our socioeconomic system in its present form. What gives me a disturbing and uneasy conscience about Ruff and Browne is their prescription.

In the first place, many of the new prophets of doom are getting rich off of other people's fears. They have developed a slick mastery of the media hype to tout their newsletters, books, lecture appearances, and private consultations at exhorbitant fees. They are commercial scribblers skilled in the art of selling. The very titles of the publications in this genre of literature are revealing: *You Can Profit from a Monetary Crisis, How to Prosper during the Coming Bad Years, How You Can Profit from the Coming Devaluation,* etc. It is not simply turning adversity into opportunity, but these "how-to" works convey almost the gleeful tenor of a waiting fly, ready to pounce on the remaining morsel once the banquet table has been deserted by the panic-stricken celebrants.

In my judgment, these writers are no different from those pious, positive, soothing chaplains to the status quo who assure their affluent followers that "God is in his heaven and all is right with the world"—so long as you think positively and harbor no negative thoughts. Both the overly optimistic and the excessively pessimistic are telling people what they want to hear—feeding and confirming their hopes and fears, their avarice and greed.

My major objection to the new breed of nay-sayers, however, springs from the social-ethics perspective. The prescription of the Ruffs and Brownes and their ilk is centered in an individualistic survival tactic—for personal safety and even prosperity. I would dub this approach "ego-ethics," which takes care of the self and one's own immediate family. There is no concern for a societal, a corporate or communal response. Look out for number one.

"God helps those who help themselves" miraculously passes as a piece of Scripture. Ignored is the authentic biblical posture: "To whom much is given, much shall be required." Store up food for yourself in some hideaway. Get your survival kit ready. Go far away from the humanity that populates the cities; go to the hills, to the rural countryside, or to small towns, and purchase land where you can till the soil.

If and when chaos abounds, how can you possibly till your own garden and let the rest of the world go by? What better example is there of self-delusion and false confidence?

These individualistic strategies for survival seem to resonate with the pioneer spirit of the frontier. The spirit of frontier individualism as the source of America's greatness was a notion supported by the scholarship of Frederick Jackson Turner. One need not adopt the Turner thesis wholeheartedly to sense the importance of the frontier in shaping the American character. In a sense, you can take the American out of the frontier, but you cannot take the frontier out of the American temperament. Despite the spirit of individualism commonly associated with the frontier, I cannot help feeling that survival in the frontier world would have been well-nigh impossible were it not for the communal spirit of coming to the aid of one's neighbor. As the poet, Alexander Pope put it:

> *By mutual confidence and mutual aid*
> *Great deeds are done and great discoveries made.*

Sheer rugged individualism, however romanticized, is self-destructive; for individuals are interdependent and both need and yearn for community. Ego-ethics has served a valued purpose in building up the nation to a high level of industrial might and power; but now that we have entered the postindustrial age, ego-ethics gets us into the pickle of profligacy.

Ego-ethics leads logically to defending yourself with rifles or machine guns, taking a sentry post to guard against or ward off intruders, and taking the law into your own hands.

I am one of those few persons who refuse to lionize the late John Wayne, folk hero of the American frontier spirit. His public image celebrated gun-slinging, rough, tough, and violent macho America. Only in America is there such utter fascination with the gun. Despite tragic assassinations of public figures, hand guns will not be outlawed but remain in the hands of outlaws—thanks to powerful lobbying efforts which appeal to the spirit of ego-ethics.

Ego-ethics is reinforced by western films, which convey an overly simple moralism that pits the "good guys" against the "bad guys" in a predictable win-lose situation. The fact is the good guys are not that good, and the bad guys are not that bad.

In a "Peanuts" cartoon strip, Lucy states the matter aptly when she remarks with theological profundity: "There is a little good and a little bad in all of us." And yet we all tend to suspend belief in our infatuation with westerns because they perpetuate our allegiance to ego-ethics.

The widespread popularity of ego-ethics and its survival techniques is reminiscent of the bomb-shelter craze that captured the public imagination in the late 1950s. The then Governor of New York Nelson Rockefeller was one of its public advocates. Ironically, private bomb shelters have been abandoned, but the armaments race and the threat of nuclear disaster have, if anything, intensified since then. Concern has faded, while the dangers of super-powerful nuclear weapons have escalated!

When I first moved to Marin County, California, in 1961, there was a bomb shelter with its concrete doorway sticking above ground just down the street from our home. During the winter time (prior to the years of drought), Marin is usually blessed with a generous downpour of rain. Everytime it rained, I could observe, the bomb shelter got flooded. And so, we drown like rats, scurrying to defend ourselves.

Ego-ethics is not only indefensible because of its undue focus on individualism, but also it is too narrow in its nationalistic, ethnocentric, and chauvinistic purview. We live in an interdependent world of the global village. Major worldwide currencies are interlocked. When Rolls Royce, operating in sterling, failed in England, it nearly bankrupted Lockheed, which operates in dollars in the United States.

Ego-ethics is reminiscent of the spirit of isolationism, which prevailed in the twenties and thirties. While that temperament was expressed in political terms, the new isolationism is to go our own way in matters of energy and other forms of wasteful consumption. The world court of public opinion is already coming down hard on our arrogant, carefree ways. Overseas, there is rising fury with Americans who consume close to 30% of the entire world's oil output. World leaders are skeptical of American intentions, since the last three presidents have vowed that U.S. oil imports would decline when they have actually risen.

No wonder the president of France remarked that American efforts to conserve energy have yet to begin. With the oil short-fall and the lack of austerity measures, the situation looks grave for the industrial nations, but even worse for the Third World developing countries. For us it means inflation eventually lead-ing to deflation, whereas for them it means facing the prospects of widespread starvation.

The realities of today's global existence call for a shift from ego-ethics to eco-ethics. The term "eco" refers to the whole inhabited earth. It also refers to an ethics that is economically and ecologically just.

While ego-ethics views the world as a lifeboat in which the rich passengers deny entry to the drowning poor, who are struggling to climb aboard, eco-ethics suggests a model of the world as a spaceship, a single, unitary community in which all are members. Eco-ethics would view the advocates of such rac-ist and genocidal policies as "triage" and "lifeboat ethics" as not simply all wet but essentially immoral, anti-humanitarian, and sub-Christian.

Garrett Hardin and William Paddock are two proponents of the "Let 'em drown, Let 'em starve" tactics with reference to the poorer nations, such as India, Pakistan, Bangladesh, and certain African countries. So long as the "have" nations are safe, secure, and satisfied with their affluence, let the "have-not" nations drown in their misery. These increasingly popular teachings among white and rich Americans should shock the humanitarian and Christian conscience. They are examples of the absurdity of ego-ethics in the face of problems that cry out for an eco-ethics response.

Eco-ethics calls for a responsible economic and environmen-tal ethic that challenges the myth that associates material pros-perity with the good life. Spaceship earth envisions a global ecology, a planetary interdependence. Those who now con-sume the lion's share of resources that are approaching the limits of their availability must face the issue of equity. The grim fact is that in only 50 years the United States has consumed more than half of the producible oil that was created by nature over the course of hundreds of millions of years. At present rates of consumption, inevitably the rest of the known supply will be exhausted.

If American consumption patterns set the pace for the rest of the world, then it is time to assume leadership in the revolution of declining expectations. God holds us accountable for the natural environment. Plundering and ravishing must give way to a care of the earth, a stewardship of the land, a love and respect for God's creation. The new eco-ethic being called for replaces the old ego-ethic of exploitation and dominion and expropriation with a posture of appreciation, reverence, and replenishment.

Eco-ethics calls for an ethic of responsibility for the whole interdependent and interconnected earth. It is a summons to collaboration with others so that we might, as E.F. Schumacher said once in a speech, "liberate ourselves from our inborn ego-centricity."

Eco-ethics calls for a closing of the widening gap between the rich nations and the poor nations through a process of sharing wealth and resources. To bear in mind the claims of eco-justice is to realize that we are our brothers' and sisters' keepers. Eco-ethics affirms that, as part of the human community, we are members of one body. All is one, and one is all. Faith seeks nothing less than a communal response, a shift from self-centered ego-ethics to eco-ethics.

Faith Seeks Simple Living: Call for Concarement

If there be merit in the medieval aphorism, "Nomen est numen" (to name is to know), then the search goes on for a felicitous expression to characterize the new ethics that transcends ego-ethics. The idea of simple living—voluntary simplicity—makes eminent sense.

There are voices from the American past—such as the Amish, the Mennonites, and the Quakers—who practice simple living as a means of bearing witness to their faith. To a nation that has faith in flux, it is remarkable how these traditions have persisted. A recent cartoon shows a long line of impatient drivers fuming and fussing, waiting to refuel their gas tanks; meanwhile, an Amish family in a horse and buggy rides serenely by, as the drivers look on ruefully from their automobiles.

Only a wasteful, arrogant, profligate people can quarrel with E. F. Schumacher's dictum that the "simple is sensible" in his *Small Is Beautiful* book. Incidentally, the ecological literature is filled with warnings that time may be running out. Schumacher delights in telling the story of the discussion at an international conference on depleting resources, when a German speaker suggested that in 70 million years, the earth's resources will be depleted and humanoids will no longer survive. To which a Japanese samurai got up, alarmed, and asked, "Sir, do you really think in 70 million years, human beings will be extinct?" The speaker replied flustered, "Oh, no, I meant to say 7 million years"—to which the Japanese scholar remarked, "Oh, thank God!"

The fact is that bigger is not necessarily better. This traditional assumption flies in the face of present-day human experience. Our schools are not pedagogically better because of their large size. They could be turning out uneducated robots, much as a factory produces buttons, if quantity supplants quality in the learning process. Sociologists tell us that the term "bureaucracy" is neutral, that bureaucracy simply refers to a rational, orderly, systematic way of conducting relatively large-scale affairs with division of labor, stipulated rules, hierarchy of administration, etc. Yet the word is more typically associated with bungling dysfunctions and waste, with red tape and distrust of large, complex structures rather than with order and neutrality. If experience denies theory, then intellectual constructs need reconstituting.

ITEM: A regional office of the Environmental Protection Agency (one of our better managed federal agencies) has a supervisor with four secretaries under his command. There is really only enough work for two of them. Come budget time, the supervisor requests two additional secretaries with the result that six persons are employed to do the job which two could handle. Can bigger be better if it is only a means by which the supervisor can enjoy more status and power and dominion?

ITEM: Every organization worth its salt—from the U.S. Army to the local school district—spends its allocated budget with a flurry when the end of the fiscal year approaches, lest its budget for the following year be diminished.

The bigger the GNP (Gross National Product), the larger the Gross National Pollution. The assumption that bigger is better may work for IBM, General Motors, and Ford—but note the anomaly that Ford actually recalled more cars than it sold in 1978. Yet any number of conglomerates that once had the urge to merge are now facing management problems and disgorging some of their once avidly sought units.

As with two other traditional axioms that have been radically transformed—"White Is Right" and "Men Are Leaders"—the time-worn shibboleth "Bigger Is Better" is being laid to rest after an illustrious career.

If not by the dictates of necessity, then by intentional design of persons, simple living is sensible. Simple living is destined to cut down on stress, fatigue, and psychic sores in our ulcer-creating world. Many harried and harassed Americans would consider giving up the yacht or the second sports car or the second color tv set for a greater measure of serenity, self-understanding, and meaning about life. "Voluntary simplicity," says a Stanford Research Institute report, "is living in a way that is outwardly simple and inwardly rich."[43]

Already there are dramatic signs, models, and paradigms emerging for simple living on a sensible scale, particularly in the ecology field. One need not flee to the rural countryside or the small town to pursue the call to simple living.

Integral Urban House was founded in Berkeley, California, in 1974 to raise the awareness of urban populations to the possibilities of ecologically sound living.[44] The house exists on an average-size urban lot, 60 feet by 140 feet. It is heated by solar energy with four flat-plate solar collectors and a thermal siphon. Its garden is put to maximal use with a luxuriant growth of corn, tomatoes, squash, cucumbers, carrots, cabbage, lettuce, peas, fruit trees, etc. The house itself is filled with a variety of alternative energy systems. The site is equipped with a gray-water recycling system, a compost in the yard—where chickens and rabbits are raised—a beehive which produces honey, and a pond for fish and crayfish. The four residents at Integral Urban House conduct seminars, workshops, and tours of the house for the public and for groups from schools and clubs. Visitors are amazed by how much can be done with so little.

Davis, California, has become a symbol of how an entire community can become energy conscious. Building construction aimed at achieving maximum energy conservation has drastically cut down on the need for air conditioners, despite the traditionally warm summer climate. Since 1973, natural gas consumption has been cut by 37% and electricity by 18%. Special bike paths and lanes were built to accommodate the community's 25,000 bicycles. Even city hall employees shuttle about on bikes to perform their duties. A fleet of double-decked London buses provides a jitney service for transportation. The clothesline is a familiar sight. Citizens in Davis seem to be alert to the call for simple living. Davis provides a viable model for improved energy efficiency, without threatening the environment, through alternative means of transportation, better insulation, conservation and solar power, and more energy-efficient household construction.

Other urban and suburban communities around the nation —such as Seattle, Washington; Hartford, Connecticut; and Northglenn, Colorado—are devising energy-saving plans to use timber wastes, to put vacant lots to use through labor-intensive growing methods—putting unemployed youth to work to provide food and curtail energy use—and to devise new wastewater treatment systems.

The idea of simple living is beautifully captured in the "Shakertown Pledge" as a covenant of the simple-living movement. For several years before I discovered who actually devised this document, I had been using it with my seminary classes and with church lay groups. I am citing the Shakertown Pledge in its entirely here in the hopes that those unfamiliar with the document will find it useful for its consciousness-raising potential.

What Would It Mean to Take the Shakertown Pledge?

Many people are attracted to the sentiments expressed, in the Shakertown Pledge, but are not sure just what the Pledge might mean in their own lives. Here is a brief discussion of each item in the Pledge:

#1. *I declare myself to be a world citizen.*

Recognizing that we are citizens of one world can have a profound impact on our daily lives. Those who make this declaration should begin to think of the needs of all the people of the earth, and adjust their lifestyle, their social vision, and their political commitments accordingly. We must go beyond our familial, village, regional, and national loyalties and extend our caring to all humankind.

#2. *I commit myself to lead an ecologically sound life.*

Through this we pledge that we will use the earth's natural resources sparingly and with gratitude. This includes the use of the land, water, air, coal, timber, oil, minerals, and other important resources. We will try to keep our pollution of the environment to a minimum and will seek wherever possible to preserve the natural beauty of the earth.

Concretely, this should mean that we will participate in local recycling efforts. It means that we will try to conserve energy and water in our own homes. It means that we will try to correct wasteful practices in our communities, schools, jobs, and in our nation.

#3. *I commit myself to lead a life of creative simplicity and to share my personal wealth with the world's poor.*

This means that we intend to reduce the frills and luxuries in our present lifestyle but at the same time emphasize the beauty and joy of living. We do this for three reasons: First, so that our own lives can be more simple and gracious, freed from excessive attachment to material goods; second, so that we are able to release more of our wealth to share with those who need the basic necessities of life; third, so that we can move toward a Just World Standard of Living in which each person shares equally in the earth's resources.

Concretely, those who take the Pledge should sit down with their families and review their present financial situation. Each item of expenditure should be looked at carefully, and funds for unnecessary or luxury items should be given to some national or international group that is working for a better standard of living for the deprived. This surplus should be a regular budgeted item from then on, and each member of the household should endeavor to see how this surplus can be increased. In the future, families and individuals who have taken the Pledge might consider meeting together in "sharing groups" to discover new ways in which community and cooperation can free up more resources for the poor.

 # 4. I commit myself to join with others in reshaping institutions in order to bring about a more just global society in which each person has full access to the needed resources for their physical, emotional, intellectual, and spiritual growth.

This complements and enhances our commitment to share our personal wealth with those who need it. Wealthy nations such as the United States need to "de-develop" those parts of their economies that are wasteful and harmful in ecological and human terms. Wealthy nations must reduce their over-consumption of scarce resources while supporting the ecologically wise development of the poor nations to the point where the basic needs of all "spaceship earth" passengers are met equally.

We commit ourselves to use our political and institutional influence toward these goals. This means that we will support those candidates who will do the most for the poor both here and abroad. It may mean that we will engage in lobbying, peaceful demonstrations, or other forms of "direct action" in support of the transfer of more of our resources and skills to the developing lands. It means that we will oppose and attempt to change those aspects of our economic system which create an unjust distribution of wealth and power here and abroad. This also means that we will support efforts to bring religious, intellectual, and vocational freedom to peoples who are being denied these basic human rights.

 # 5. I commit myself to occupational accountability, and in so doing I will seek to avoid the creation of products which cause harm to others.

This most certainly means that we will not allow our labor to go into making products which kill others. It should also mean that we will take a close look at what we are producing to determine if it is safe and is ecologically sound. We should also consider our choice of a career and whether or not it contributes concretely to a better world for all humankind. If our present occupation does not do so, or is only marginally helpful to others, we may decide to change it, even if we earn less money as a result.

#6. I affirm the gift of my body and commit myself to its proper nourishment and physical well being.

Many of us in the developed (or "overdeveloped") countries desecrate the "temple" of our own bodies through overeating or through consuming physically harmful and nutritionally "empty" foods. Also, through our meat-centered diets we consume protein (see *Diet for a Small Planet*, by Frances Lappé, Ballentine Paperbacks).

Serious attention to this point would mean: 1. A commitment to maintain our weight at the normal healthy level. 2. A reduction in the consumption of animal protein in our diets. 3. Regular attention to healthy physical exercise. 4. A reduction in consumption of empty calories, especially in desserts, candy, pastries, alcohol, and other food products which have great amounts of refined sugar.

#7. I commit myself to examine continually my relations with others and to attempt to relate honestly, morally, and lovingly to those around me.

We will seek to understand and improve our relationships with others and to treat each person as our neighbor. We will try to affirm and nurture the gifts and talents of others. We support the development of the small group and face-to-face community in religious life—since here many people are learning new ways to communicate their love, their needs, their hopes and dreams, and their anguish. Small groups and communities have also been helpful in enabling people to see more clearly how they affect others.

#8. I commit myself to personal renewal through prayer, meditation, and study.

For many people, "prayer" and "meditation" are alternate terms for the same process of turning one's thoughts toward God. We believe that deep and continuing personal renewal can result from a discipline of prayer or meditation, and from reading and reflection. We encourage each person to find his or her own individual spiritual discipline and practice it regularly. For a start, we suggest setting aside time twice a day for prayer or meditation.

#9. I commit myself to responsible participation in a community of faith.

We believe that God not only has a relationship with each of us individually, but also collectively—as a people. One of the obligations—and joys—of living our faith is that we are called to worship together with others. We recognize that common worship and the support of a community of common beliefs are essential to an active, creative, joyous life. Concretely, this means participation in a church or synagogue, a "house church," or other worship group.

****

Signing the Pledge:

Taking the Pledge simply means that you agree with the substance of the nine points that we have proposed, and that you want to join with us in a common community of support. The "Shakertown Pledge Group" is a loosely knit association of people who hold the principles of the Pledge in common and who are attempting to redirect their lives toward creative simplicity and are working for a more just global society.

The Shakertown Pledge was written to appeal to a broad audience composed of all people of faith. We encourage people from specific religious traditions to consider writing your own pledge, in language that may be more uniquely suited to the language and practices of your community. (San Francisco Group, "Simple Living Project," 2160 Lake Street, San Francisco 94121. National Office: The Shakertown Pledge Group, West 44th and York South, Minneapolis, Minn. 55410.)

In using the Shakertown Pledge as a teaching tool, the first question I ask a group is, "How many of you are willing to sign this pledge right now?" In a group of 15 persons, perhaps 4 or 5 respond affirmatively. The next question is, "Which items are the most difficult for you to subscribe to?" Then, "Which items are the easiest for you to agree with?" I have usually been impressed with the candor of the discussion that follows.

The idea is not to cultivate a "holier-than-thou" attitude or to coerce or intimidate everyone into a common mold, but rather to start the reflection and action process toward finding meaning and fulfillment in life not solely through material means. We can all make do with much less, when we realize that how we live affects the way others live, when we realize that the sheer scale of our eating, drinking, and consuming habits may actually be harmful to our health and detrimental to others.

As Adam Finnerty writes, what the Shakertown Pledge designers had in mind is not a "St. Francis trip" of "holy poverty," or even a miserly notion of frugality.[45] What is envisioned is a creative simplicity that blends personal piety, social conscience, and a simple life style. The idea is to reappraise our life style in the light of our faith and from the perspective of the rest of the world, and not simply from the vantage point of our own self-centered wants.

Responses to the Shakertown Pledge have taken many forms. Some groups take the pledge with political action in mind and seek to change the structures of injustice on a global basis. One current focus is to call multinational corporations to task for exploitative or oppressive practices, particularly in the Third World. Action may involve lobbying, boycotts of products, shareholders' resolutions, litigation, or consultations with management. Recent social action projects have centered in the boycott of Nestlé products and in the protest against companies that support apartheid as a social system in South Africa. Other groups work on issues of affirmative action and equal opportunity in employment.

Another response deals more in the area of ecology and life style changes. Group discussions of the Shakertown Pledge often center around ecological issues. Frequently the objection surfaces that the tone is too stringent, something like the "hard sayings" of the Sermon on the Mount. I have outlined a list of simpler, perhaps less demanding, items in the course of these discussions as a basis for dialogue. The following list—which I hesitate to call "Lee's Pledge"—is indicative of specific steps that may be adopted by those who are seeking to pursue the way of simple living:

1. Walk or ride a bicycle whenever possible, especially for short errands to mail a letter or go to the bank. Why not feel the spring in your leg muscles and laugh all the way to the bank?

2. Exercise regularly to keep your body fit by jogging, playing tennis, body movement exercises, swimming, or some other enjoyable sport you can take up with a friend or a significant other. I find the tennis court to be a congenial place for exercise and fellowship—lots of love and service, but no mercy!

3. Cut down on electrical usage by turning off all unnecessary lights that are carelessly left burning at home or at work place. Large homes and office buildings usually have many lights left on. In many other nations entire rooms in the house are devoid of heat and light unless they are in actual use.

4. Lower the thermostat during the cold season and raise it during the summer, if air conditioning is being used. Wear warmer clothing such as sweaters and vests during the winter and cool, informal attire during the summer.

5. Eat less meat; substitute cheese, fish, poultry, beans, nuts, etc. The book *Diet for a Small Planet* by Frances Moore Lappé gives a good analysis of international food waste through meat-oriented diets and argues for an alternative grain-centered diet. It also lists numerous recipes that are both tasty and nutritional.

6. Plan meal preparation to use oven heat more efficiently. By careful planning, for example, a casserole, dessert, and potatoes can be cooked with the same oven heat.

7. Plan weekly menus around sale items at stores. By following newspaper advertisements, one can plan the shopping, instead of resorting to impulse buying. Avoid being a junk-food junkie. Stop paying extra for attractive and colorful packaging when you can purchase food that is less expensive and more nutritious. Buy store-brand items, instead of nationally advertised brands.

8. Recycle used articles, such as furniture and clothing, by donating to and buying at thrift shops. The amount and quality of discarded items that can be put to good use in our "disposable society" is truly amazing. When I informed my class that nearly all of my clothing is bought at the seminary's thrift shop, one of the students quipped, "It looks that way." He barely passed the course! Recycle tin, glass, newspapers, and water from the bath.

9. Grow, can, and freeze your own fruits and vegetables (if yard space is available for growing). Buy fruits and vegetables that are in season.

10. Compost your organic garbage with leaves to be used as fertilizer for your own vegetable garden (if you have space available).

11. Share your resources with others at the local and global levels. Share your table with guests and contribute to overseas needs and involvement through programs that foster eco-justice on a global basis and that strive for the just use of world resources.

12. Resist the consumer urge to buy things. Life's meaning and satisfaction is not dependent upon being immersed in a sea of material things. Captivity to consumerism inhibits our freedom and misplaces our priorities in life. I was interested to hear that an organization called "Save Our Resources" has emerged to help consumers resist the buying mania. This group distributes a card which reads as follows:

> **SAVE OUR RESOURCES**
> Don't Buy It!
> Call our volunteers when you feel
> compelled to buy something.
> We can talk you out of buying!

A phone number is given with appropriate hours for calling. On the other side, the card advises:

> **DON'T BUY—**
> Instead:
> —Ask a friend for it.
> —Borrow or share it.
> —Get it used or make it.
> —Live without it!

13. If you use a credit card, such as Visa, Mastercard, Sears, or American Express, make full payments on or before the due date and avoid the interest charges.

14. Borrow money only when absolutely necessary. Avoid indebtedness if possible. If you are heavily in debt, devise a systematic program to work down your excess to a reasonable and prudent level. If you simply cannot handle debt, but become its victim, then learn to bid farewell to the "wonderful world of credit."

Now I would be the first to concede that the idea of a simpler life style—whether embodied in the Shakertown Pledge or in the sensible 14 points listed above—seems like a midget-sized response to a gigantic problem of excessive debt and credit. Of course, by itself, such a commitment will not be a panacea and is not intended to be. However, the concept points up the kind of attitudinal changes needed wherein *perspectives*—or percepts—precede precepts, wherein priorities are questioned and reordered. What is called for is more in the nature of taking a step in the right direction or lighting a candle in the darkness instead of cursing at the darkness.

Moreover, it stands to reason that if more Americans were to consume less, if we were to adopt a lowered level of expectations, we would be resisting the temptation to chase prices up —and thereby diminish the pressures on the "demand-pull" type of inflation. As an added dividend, we would be contributing to the pool of savings, which would provide a sounder basis for capital formation and investment. From the standpoint of spaceship earth and of global justice, Americans would be less guilty of gobbling up such a disproportionate share of the earth's depletable resources. From a global perspective, it is not expecting too much for rich Americans to live simply so that others might simply live. Indeed, to whom much is given, much is expected.

I want to affirm simple living as the sound, sane, and sensible wave of the future. On the conceptual level, however, my reservation is that simple living may become associated with simple-mindedness, or at least with naive, illusory, and romantic notions. Never mind the fact that our present suicidal course of spending and consumerism is subject to the same charges. After all, we *are* a sophisticated, modern, powerful society, not a simple, backward village—so goes the argument.

What other concept could be mustered? I recall with nostalgia—the anguish having receded into history—that when I was studying for my graduate German examination, I was impressed by how German scholars could coin new words almost out of thin air to discuss old realities. Again, *nomen est numen.* The term I am seeking to coin really brings together three feelings or vibrations or modes of awareness: care, concern, and commitment.

Care is a deep and sensitive feeling, but it is also a prerequisite for life. We think of care in the sense of nurture of the newborn baby, caring in response to the infant's needs. Then there are the "care packages," which are symbolic of the humanitarian spirit that renders aid in crisis and emergency situations. During the hunger crisis that affected about 20% of the population in Greater Seattle between 1970 and 1972, when Boeing sneezed and nearly gave the community pneumonia, the residents of Greater Seattle were grateful recipients of care packages—from Japan!

An ego-ethics that is centered around self lacks a caring spirit. It is essentially narcissistic, which is self-destructive. Recall the myth of Narcissus recounted by the poet Ovid. Narcissus has a fatal flaw: a fierce pride that prevents him from returning anyone's affection. The Goddess Retribution causes Narcissus to be smitten with an overpowering self-infatuation. Worn out by repeated efforts to touch and kiss his own reflection in the River Styx, he falls in and drowns. Even in death, Narcissus continues for eternity the frustrated infatuation with his own reflected image.

Christopher Lasch, historian at the University of Rochester, discerns a new spirit of narcissism in American society. Lasch feels that people of narcissistic bent are eminently well suited to life in bureaucratic settings. They tend to rise to leadership posts in corporations, political organizations, government agencies, religious organizations, and just about any other bureau-cracy. They sit high in the saddle of society, and their style permeates our culture.

In the new spirit of narcissism, many Americans care only for themselves. In this connection, they become carefree spenders, spendthrifts on a creditholic binge, who squander away their assets on things that aren't needed. In matters of social responsibility, the noncaring attitude proudly snaps, "I don't give a damn." Bumper stickers that read "Give a Damn" reflect the call to care.

Another dimension of caring is captured in the biblical idea of stewardship. Human beings are seen as caretakers, as stew-ards who take care of God's creation—the land, the people, the earth and all that dwells within it. (Ps. 24:1) Therefore, we are not to make idols of material possessions and worship them. Ultimately they are not ours; they are merely entrusted to our care. To care fully is to be fully human.

Concern is a second ingredient that points to the thrust we are groping after. Like caring, concern is a deep-seated human emotion that is essential for the human community. Without it, the commonweal would be impoverished and imperiled. The lack of concern is not only callousness, but also blindness. Such hardness of heart and shortness of sight are aptly portrayed in the Parable of the Good Samaritan (Luke 10:30–37). When they came upon a naked, wounded, and half-dead victim of robbers on the road to Jericho, many passed by on the other side of the road—including a priest and a tax collector. But the Samaritan had compassion. He bound up the wounds, took the injured party to an inn, paid the innkeeper, and promised to return and pay whatever additional sums were necessary. Compassion, along with mercy and empathy, is the depth dimension of con-cern. "Go and do likewise," instructs Jesus.

A modern-day, Jericho-Road tragedy, referred to by ethi-cists as the "Kew Gardens principle," happened in Kew Gar-dens, Queens, New York. A young woman was brutally beaten in front of a large, middle-class housing project. Her screams for help were met by hundreds of windows being closed and shades being drawn. Those who lack concern wait in darkness and will never see the light.

To have concern is to know pathos, to sense the feelings of the heart of which the rational mind has but scant comprehension. To be concerned is to be aware, to have our consciousness raised, to have our minds blown, to be open to change and willing to accept new mandates.

Care and concern lead to a third component: *Commitment.* Commitment presupposes awareness. As the sense of awareness grows, say, to replenish the earth—to "dress, till, and keep the earth"—the yearning is to move from apathy to awareness to action. Commitment is the loyalty and passion that spring from compassion. Without the sense of commitment, there is aimlessness or apathy, moral and spiritual drifting. Without commitment, analysis, models, and paradigms become academic, an indoor sport of mental gymnastics for the contentment of intellectual snobs. Without commitment, philosophers may dissect the world, but never change it. Commitment is the fulcrum for change.

Commitment implies conviction, something worthy to cherish, some high goal or aspiration to believe in and, if necessary, to die for. To rephrase Plato's famous dictum: "The unexamined life is not worth living." The uncommitted life is not worth having; for the uncommitted life is the unlived life.

Consider the obvious contempt the author of the Book of Revelation must have felt toward the uncommitted when he wrote: "I know your works: you are neither cold nor hot. . . . So, because you are lukewarm, and neither cold nor hot, I will spew you out of my mouth." (Rev. 3:15–16)

We are so accustomed to sitting and waiting for the good things in life to be invented, manufactured, mass produced, packaged, and shipped to our friendly neighborhood store for us to purchase on credit that we expect goals, purposes, and ideals to come that way too. The committed person is not waiting, but is in the searching mood. We cannot find God, or even know that God is waiting for us, unless we go out and search.

The Christian is called to commitment—to responsible action in the human community, to act with care, concern, and commitment for the sake of love and justice. Hence, the concept I am coining is *concarement.*

So we are led to an ethics of concarement—which brooks no excuse for retreat into an inner world of the private self-centered self, all wrapped up in one's own self-preservation. Concarement will not tolerate a moral cop-out or a removal from collective, communal, and corporate involvements.

The call to concarement affirms that there is yet time to turn away from immersion in material splendor, to be freed from excessive attachment to things, to look away from hedonistic self-preoccupation in order to turn to goals that are worthy of the spirit of concarement.

In a sense, the call to an ethics of concarement seems hopelessly otherworldly and wholly unrealistic to a generation that worships its own created artifacts. It is quite possible that the really real seems false, whereas the really false or illusory surrogates have become real. Here is an inversion of values, a pathology of normalcy—wherein our consumer-oriented life has become so pathological that human beings are innoculated from the recognition of reality. We have become immune from the experience of authenticity. If our entire way of life is founded on pathological premises, that bodes ill for its continued viability.

If the life style of voluntary simplicity were to be adopted, it would have the impact of curtailing consumer consumption, cutting down on the demand for debt and credit, cooling off the roaring rate of inflation, and contributing to the increased level of personal savings.

Alas, complex economic problems seem to defy simple solutions. Many variables are at play, so that overemphasis upon one set of salient variables could ignite unwelcomed developments elsewhere. Moreover, while not ignoring worldwide implications, much of our focus has centered on the domestic scene. We must also keep a wary eye fixed on international economic developments—especially the significance that lies behind the gyrating price of gold, the erratic fluctuations of the dollar, the

OPEC cartel's oil price hikes, the new vulnerability to disruptions of oil supply, and the mammoth supply of hot money floating around the globe in the form of Eurodollars. Any one or a combination of these variables could spark trouble.

If simple living is pushed too far—not a clear and present danger at this time, given our materialistic cultural climate— the critic might charge that this could plunge the economy into a recession and increase unemployment. To take an extreme example, if the public were to buy only half of the cars Detroit produces, there would be trouble not just in "Motor City," but throughout the nation, because the $350-billion auto industry comprises 18.5% of our GNP and is tied in with hundreds of suppliers. Surely there is a problem here of reallocation of resources. It would be possible for Detroit (with a little ingenuity) to redirect its energies to other products—such as buses, mass-transit facilities, or battery-operated cars—to take up the slack. Industries have successfully changed over from war productions to peacetime products. Airplane manufacturers, for example, have achieved a better mix between defense-related and commercial aircraft.

As much as business complains about government regulations, the federal requirements for better mileage standards have actually helped Detroit to respond to public tastes for fuel-efficient cars in the "OPEC Age" and to compete more adequately with foreign imports. Instead of continuing to churn out gas guzzlers, it is better to endure short-term, temporary dislocations than to suffer the fatality of a wholesale collapse in pursuit of a suicidal course.

Simple living is not intended to be an absolute social-ethics response to a massive problem. It is more in tune with the thinking of Reinhold Niebuhr, perhaps the most influential religious thinker in American history. Niebuhr eschewed quick-fix solutions and utopian answers because of their endemic oversimplification and illusions. Amidst the complexities of economic and sociopolitical decisions, we do best to settle for what Niebuhr has called "tolerable harmonies" and "proximate justice."

Hence, our approach should be to achieve a better balance, to correct the excesses, abuses, and distortions of inflation, debt, consumerism, and diminished productivity—lest these excesses lead to collapse. To achieve a saner and more tolerable balance between low savings and low productivity, on the one hand, and high inflation and overextended credit, on the other hand, does not necessarily mean a swing clear over to the other extreme of recession, high unemployment, excessive production resulting in inventory gluts, and workaholism. A recovery of the Puritan ethic of thrift would check the trends toward undersaving and overspending. Such a reversal would restore a better balance and make for a healthier economy.

Economic life and ethical life are not lived in the heavenly, idyllic Garden of Eden or in the fiery Inferno that is the city of hell. They exist in the tension between these two extremes. They are lived between the point and the counterpoint—always striving to achieve a just and tolerable harmony. We may say with the poet William Wordsworth that our path is clarified only "with an eye made quiet by the power of harmony and the deep power of joy."

The appeal to simple living, the shift from ego-ethics to eco-ethics, the call to concarement is an antidote to the excessive consumer-buying binge, the overextended creditholic impulse. It says with Henry David Thoreau: "Money is not required to buy one necessity of the soul." It shouts a loud "Amen!" to the late Margaret Mead, when she mused: "Prayer does not use any artificial energy; it doesn't burn up any fossil fuel; it doesn't pollute. Neither does song . . . love . . . the dance."[46]

Faith Seeks Judgment and Hope

We dwell among a profligate people, a people of unclean lips, who have strayed, like the Prodigal Son, far from the Puritan virtues of frugality, simplicity, honesty, thrift, and industry.

In our love affair with credit and debit financing at all levels of spending, we have piled debt upon debt in pyramidal fashion. We are a self-indulgent, hedonistic, extravagant people,

who consume the earth's depleting resources indiscriminately
—while the majority of the world's population lives on a subsist-
ence basis at the edge of poverty.

Judgment is coming from many quarters to warn us that our
economy is careening headlong out of control, heading on a
collision course with calamity. Dr. Benjamin A. Rogge of Wa-
bash College characterizes the person in our economy's driver's
seat as "a well-meaning drunk, taking more drinks, driving a
wrecked car, along a strange road, being buffeted by strong
winds, and likely to spin out of control."[47]

Most bankers seem to be congenitally optimistic. They tend
to exude confidence and reassure the public. Surely it is unlike
them to express Cassandra-like gobs of gloom. It, therefore,
comes as a surprise when the staid chief economist of the Bank
of America, Walter E. Hoadley, tells an audience of financial
analysts that "disaster may end Americans' extravagance," and
that it may take an "economic Pearl Harbor for Americans to
change their profligate ways." (Of course, from the perspective
of faith, one could argue that anything which puts an end to
extravagance and profligacy should be viewed as a blessing,
rather than a "disaster.") Hoadley's scenario includes the inevi-
tability of wage-and-price controls, which will be lifted 6 to 18
months after they have been in force, and "then inflation will
take off and really be out of control."[48]

We are depleting our capital base in nonrenewable resources at an alarming rate. Meanwhile, our garbage grows in
ever-increasing volume. Taking little thought for the future,
most Americans do not recycle in earnest, or compost, or cut
down on consumption, or insist on less packaging. Waste is not
being used for fuel or fertilizer.

It is difficult to change old habits and accustomed ways and
to move from knowing the truth to doing it. In the last week,
how many of us who needed to go a short distance have walked,
ridden a bike, car pooled, or taken public transportation? How
many of us will recycle cans, bottles, and papers for a brief
period, but then slack off with the comforting thought that our
neighbor is good at such things. Inertia, neglect, taking the easy

way out, soon we find ourselves lapsing back to our old profligate ways.

We need to be reminded of the dinosaur's plight—and fate. During the Mesozoic Era—from about 225 to 65 million years ago—the mighty dinosaur stalked the earth. The word *dinos* comes from the Greek and means "terrible." Indeed, dinosaurs were terrible and terrifying. Many larger ones stood 20 feet high and had skulls 4 feet long with huge, daggerlike teeth. Some were 80 feet long and weighed 85 tons! In fact, the most recent dinosaur bone found by paleontologist James A. Jensen in Dry Mesa Quarry, southwest of Delta, Colorado, was a shoulder blade that belonged to a monster so tall it could look over a five-story building. The 140-million-year-old fossil—dubbed "ultrasaurus"—is about 50 to 60 feet tall and 75 to 80 feet long. Needless to say, the dinosaur was a proud and powerful beast who dominated the landscape. Yet at the very height of its powers, it became extinct and vanished from the face of the earth—leaving only fossils for future scientists to study.

Scientists have long been puzzled by the demise of the gigantic dinosaur, wondering how something so powerful could disappear so completely. The best guess is that large mountain ranges emerged, taking the place of the vast swamplands, from whence dinosaurs derived much of their food. These changes drastically altered the climate and food supply. Having been locked into their erstwhile comfortable and compatible conditions, dinosaurs were simply unable to adjust and adapt to the new challenges of the changed environment. Extinction became their fate.

Thus far our account of the dinosaur has been as factual as is warranted by the available scientific evidence. Now to move to a parable. With the dinosaur's demise came the great ascent of a feeble, frail, and frightened creature, who suddenly stood erect and scanned the earth with an assurance of personal safety and social security. This creature in the chain of being is called man/woman.

Man/woman was enabled to flourish because of a capacity to adapt, to wonder, to imagine, to dream dreams and see visions, to be free and flexible, to be inventive and innovative, to be creative even in the face of adversity and against seemingly insuperable odds. That capacity was and continues to be our promise and our salvation!

Note the significance of the parable of the dinosaur in relation to our current challenges: If we are so locked into our accustomed and comforting life styles, if we refuse to adapt and change our profligate ways, we are doomed to extinction. We will be known by our fossils! If we are judged and found wanting, we will have deserved our fate.

In the Old Testament, the Book of Deuteronomy depicts a certain prophetic philosophy of history that has led to varied accounts and even misinterpretations. The catchy equation, "Piety pays and perversity is punished," is surely oversimplified. Nevertheless, the key idea presented by Deuteronomy is a stern rebuke, a harsh judgment, a promised punishment, which will be exercised by God's wrath.

Deuteronomy is first and foremost a positive program for justice, an invitation to a covenantal relationship, which the people are free to adopt or to reject. If they adopt the course of justice, there is the promise of abundance. Prosperity will be their lot. They will experience the "Shalom" of God, which is a blend of peace and prosperity. To adopt justice, though, means to maximize the ways by which wealth and resources are to be distributed and shared—while minimizing the concentration of wealth in the hands of an elite few, a privileged power elite. If justice is adopted, the people may expect "to eat, be sated, give thanks and rejoice." To accept justice is to choose life.

However, if the people's choice is rejection of the program for justice, if injustices are callously perpetrated, then surely the curse will follow, for the people have chosen death. It will come in the form of plague, pestilence, drought, fever, mildew, itch, the fall of the political structure (monarchy), and the collapse of the economy. Indeed, the list of curses is excruciatingly lengthy and specific: Cursed will be the cities, the fields, the food baskets (supermarkets?), the fruit of the land. The Lord will curse the people with madness and blindness and astonishment of heart. They shall be lost souls, groping in the darkness (Deut. 28).

What God has freely given—a land that flows with milk and honey—God can swiftly take away from an undeserving people. The people of God have an option: to choose life or death, blessing or cursing. Those who reject the blessing will embrace the curse. "Therefore, choose life," implores the prophet. (Deut. 30:19) The judgment of God is "like the growling of a lion," but God's mercy is "like dew upon the grass." (Proverbs 19:12)

To rich and prosperous America, the harsh word of the prophet is indeed chastening: Beware "lest, when you have eaten and are full, and have built goodly houses and live in them, and when your herds and flocks multiply, and your silver and gold is multiplied, and all that you have is multiplied, then your heart be lifted up, and you forget the LORD your God. . . . Beware lest you say in your heart, 'My power and the might of my hand have gotten me this wealth.' " (Deut. 8:12–17)

A similarly stinging rebuke is found in the Parable of the Rich Fool which Jesus tells:

> "The land of a rich man brought forth plentifully; and he thought to himself, 'What shall I do, for I have nowhere to store my crops?' And he said, 'I will do this: I will pull down my barns, and build larger ones; and there I will store all my grain and my goods. And I will say to my soul, Soul, you have ample goods laid up for many years; take your ease, eat, drink, be merry.' But God said to him, 'Fool! This night your soul is required of you; and the things you have pre-pared, whose will they be?' So is he who lays up treasure for himself, and is not rich toward God." (Luke 12:16–21)

All of us can feel the sting of the rebukes by Jesus and the Deuteronomist. For we are all close cousins to the Rich Fool; we all have forgotten the source of our strength and sustenance. We are all proud of our possessions and connoisseurs in cultivat-ing the fine art of taking it easy; Drink, eat, and be merry. We are rich in material things, but not rich towards God. Perhaps there is no fool worse than a rich fool, who can build bigger and better barns, who can flaunt his or her accumulated wealth in conspicuous display. And yet, we are reminded, it is possible to gain the whole material world and lose one's soul.

The day of judgment is at hand! Unless we mend our ways, there is an inescapable retribution for our excesses, our profligacy, our injustices, our indulgence in the face of world-wide human need. As we choose, so we are chosen.

Not only does faith demand judgment, but hope is also en-demic to the story of faith. Christian hope is a perennial theme for the panorama of faith, which embraces the memory of God's intrusion into human history through Christ and hope for the future consummation of history in the Kingdom of God. Chris-tian faith relates memory to promise in a present historical arena.

To hope is to be so imbued with a sense of Divine Discontent that one is deeply motivated to fuse present-day realities with future possibilities. Hope brings with it the anticipation of new-ness of life, the prospects of a new birth and a new creation.

Buckminster Fuller employs a memorable parable of hope as born from newness of life when he refers to the unborn chick being nurtured and supported in the warm and comforting environment of the egg. There comes a time, however, when the chick exhausts the support system within that closed envi-ronment and will die unless it pecks its way through the shell and realizes newness of life.

Fuller's parable has application for our present malaise as this contemporary visionary goes on to draw these implications:

> My own picture of humanity today finds us just about to step out from amongst the pieces of our just one-second-ago broken eggshell. Our innocent, trial-and-error-sustain-ing nutriment is exhausted. We are faced with an entirely new relationship to the universe. We are going to have to spread our wings of intellect and fly or perish; that is, we must dare immediately to fly by the generalized principles governing the universe and not by the ground rules of yesterday's superstitions and erroneously conditioned reflexes.[49]

And so the future summons us to fly on our own wings into the new creation.

The sense of hope is spoken of by the prophets and apostles with reference to the new. Hope points us toward newness of life. Thus the Old Testament speaks of the New Exodus, the New Conquest, the New Zion, the New Jerusalem. Also, the New Testament points to the New Covenant, the New Life, the New Commandments, the New Heaven, and the New Earth. The God of Promise and the God of Resurrection are symbols of hope.

Christian hope is an essential part of the treasure we have in earthen vessels. The church has a mandate to proclaim the message of hope that Jesus Christ is Lord, and the church's mission is to bear witness to this hope—especially in a time of despair and hopelessness, when all seems lost. When financial panic hits and people are losing their heads, that's the time to keep the faith in the knowledge that Jesus Christ is the same yesterday, today, and tomorrow. As the Apostle Paul wrote: "We are afflicted in every way, but not crushed; perplexed, but not driven to despair; persecuted, but not forsaken; struck down, but not destroyed. . . ." Continues Paul, "So do not lose heart. . . . For this slight momentary affliction is preparing for us an eternal weight of glory beyond all comparison, because we look not to the things that are seen but to the things that are unseen; for the things that are seen are transient, but the things that are unseen are eternal." (2 Cor. 4:8–9, 16–18)

We do, indeed, hope for what we do not see. We also hope to be able to discern clearly the things that can be seen. And we hope for the summer that surely follows our winter of discontent. A hope that is active and realistic begins with an identification and delineation of our problem. Authentic hope emerges from the depths of deep despair.

The late great philosophical journalist Walter Lippman regarded the erosion of human hope in our day as our greatest human tragedy. If that is so, then our legacy of Christian hope in the love and justice of God is our greatest human asset. Without hope, as without vision, the people perish.

The New Testament witness of Christian hope looks forward to the Lordship of Christ as God's Messiah both today and in the days to come, both in our time and in the time to come. This hope is both horizontal—relating to the here and now, to the present tense—and also vertical—with reference to the end of time, to future eschatalogical time.

The biblical story of Noah and the flood speaks of God's judgment upon the whole earth, but not as final demise or a total wipe-out. Rather, the key to the story opens up the prospects of a New Beginning, of newness of life, following the disaster.

One of the most important books I read as a young person growing up in 1946, and still recall vividly, was the novel by George R. Stewart entitled *Earth Abides.* Later on I learned that that phrase came from the Book of Ecclesiastes in the Old Testament. The novel is set in the San Francisco Bay area following a nuclear bomb explosion. Everything is decaying; the large buildings have been torn to shreds; the bridges are hanging grotesquely; various insects and animals have invaded the land; chaos and disorder are pervasive. Suddenly, far from the ruins, a man emerges from the Berkeley hills. Then a woman wanders down from the Oakland hills. Man and woman meet. Earth abides. That is our perennial hope.

Hope is that special vision which sees above and beyond the present despair and frustration. In the Book of Jeremiah (32: 6–15), the prophet seems to be advising his people to buy land, to invest in real estate, calling it their "redemption." His counsel is not investment advice for would-be real-estate tycoons. Redemption in this context means to save the land from going into bankruptcy; that is, to keep the property within the family as a birthright or an inheritance.

The paramount point of Jeremiah in counseling purchase of the land is to serve as a symbol of hope, faith, and confidence. Jeremiah is looking ahead to the time after the fall of the monarchy. He is insisting that all is not lost. Take heart, have faith, be of good cheer, for after the fall, there will be better days ahead; there will be a restoration of confidence. As the Letter to the

Hebrews expresses it: "Do not throw away your confidence, which has a great reward." (Heb. 10:35)

Surely this message needs to be sounded today as a note of hope to a beleaguered people who see a bleak future ahead. If the credit binge and the excesses of the inflationary funny-money game should run our economy into a titanic "bust," that will not be the end—in the sense of *finis,* or a period. It will only be a semicolon, or an end with a *telos,* a purposful end to enable newness of life.

However painful, excessive debt and credit must be liquidated sooner or later, if not voluntarily, then by forces beyond control. From our eco-ethics perspective, the pain should be shared.

Christian hope leads us to the bold assertion that the world will not be coming to an end with an economic collapse. The world will be coming to a New Beginning!

The Great Seal of the United States, which is displayed on the once-mighty dollar bill, carries this motto: *"Novus Ordo Seclorum"*—or, roughly translated, "A New Age Begins." That was the hope of our founding fathers. That continues to be our hope. Welcome to the threshold of the New Age!

Notes

1. *The Bank Credit Analyst,* March, 1978, p. 36.
2. Robert L. Heilbroner, *An Inquiry into the Human Prospect* (New York: W. W. Norton, 1974), pp. 17–18.
3. Robert Nisbet, *Twilight of Authority* (New York: Oxford University Press, 1975).
4. Robert de Fremery, "Banking Reforms to Stop Periodic Liquidity Crises," *The Commercial and Financial Chronicle,* July 9, 1970, p. 1.
5. Quoted in "U.S. Bank Loans Abroad Stirring Concern," *New York Times,* January 15, 1976.
6. As of March, 1980, mortgage rates had risen to more than 17%, and loans were difficult to secure.
7. Peter Drucker, "Towards a New Form of Money?" *The Wall Street Journal,* June 28, 1979.
8. George C. Edwards, *Money* (Berkeley: Wetzel Brothers, 1923), p. 62.
9. Ibid.
10. Ibid.
11. I have sought to condense and simplify Exter's views. He has not written extensively, save for memoranda. Those who wish more complex details should search out the article by John Exter entitled "Money in Today's World," in *Champions of Freedom,* ed. Barbara J. Smith (Hillsdale, Mich.: Hillsdale College Press, 1975).
12. Quoted in *The Wall Street Journal,* August 25, 1978.
13. George Finlay, *History of Greece* (London: Oxford University Press, 1877), p. 432.
14. Andrew Dickson White, *Fiat Money Inflation in France* (1912; reprint ed., Irvington-on-Hudson, N.Y.: The Foundation for Economic Education, 1959), pp. 113–16.
15. Ibid., p. 58.
16. Ibid., pp. 58–59.
17. Elgin Groseclose, *Money: The Human Conflict* (Norman, Okla.: University of Oklahoma Press, 1934), p. 245.
18. John Kenneth Galbraith, *The Great Crash, 1929* (Boston: Houghton Mifflin, 1961), p. 113.

19. Ibid., p. 105.
20. Ibid., p. 75.
21. Ibid., p. 127.
22. Ibid., p. 124.
23. Ibid., p. 143.
24. Franklin W. Ryan, *The Internal Debts of the United States* (New York, 1933), p. 321.
25. Samuel C. Kincheloe, *Research Memorandum on Religion in the Depression* (New York: Social Science Research Council, 1937); and Robert T. Handy, "The American Religious Depression," *Church History,* March, 1960.
26. Robert T. Handy, *A History of the Churches in the United States and Canada* (Oxford: Oxford University Press, 1979), pp. 379–80.
27. James B. Shuman and David Rosenau, *The Kondratieff Wave* (New York: World Publishing, 1972).
28. O. V. Wells, "The Depression of 1873–79," *Agricultural History* 11 (1937).
29. Cited in Freeman Tilden, *A World in Debt* (New York: Funk and Wagnalls, 1936), p. 141.
30. For an analysis of the career and marital problems facing middle-aged couples, see Robert Lee and Marjorie Casebier, *The Spouse Gap: Weathering the Marriage Crisis during Middlescence* (New York: Abingdon Press, 1971).
31. A Boston research organization, Harbridge House, conducted a study of the impact of foreign import cars on the American economy and concluded with this startling finding: In 1977, the average fuel efficiency of all imported cars operating in the U.S. was 32 miles per gallon; whereas, the average for all U.S.-built cars was 13 miles per gallon. If American cars had been as efficient as the foreign makes, "we would not have needed to import any crude oil to meet American gasoline requirements." (*Honolulu Star-Bulletin,* March 30, 1980.)
32. Studs Terkel, *Working* (New York: Random House, Pantheon Books, 1974), p. xi.
33. Ibid., p. xxiv.
34. "Work in America," Report of the Upjohn Institute, 1973, p. 4.
35. Quoted in *Newsweek,* January 1, 1973, p. 48.
36. Robert Lee, *Religion and Leisure in America: A Study in Four Dimensions* (New York: Abingdon Press, 1964); Wayne Oates, *Confessions of a Workaholic: The Facts about Work Addiction* (New York: Abingdon Press, 1972).
37. Quoted in Ralph Barton Perry, *Puritanism and Democracy* (New York: Vanguard Press, 1944), p. 307.
38. Cited in *Work in America,* Report of a Special Task Force to the

Secretary of Health, Education and Welfare (Cambridge, Mass.: MIT Press, 1973), p. 22.

39. See Douglas McGregor, *The Human Side of Enterprise* (New York: McGraw-Hill, 1960).

40. James M. Gustafson, *Christian Ethics and the Community* (Philadelphia: Pilgrim Press, 1971), pp. 154–57.

41. James S. Dusenberry, *Money and Credit Impact and Control* (Englewood Cliffs, N.J.: Prentice-Hall, 1972), p. 3.

42. For a fuller discussion, see Walter Guzzardi, Jr., "The New Down-to-Earth Economics," *Fortune,* December 31, 1978.

43. Reported in *San Francisco Chronicle,* October 26, 1977.

44. See *The Integral Urban House: Self-Reliant Living in the City* (San Francisco: Sierra Club Books, 1979).

45. Adam D. Finnerty, *No More Plastic Jesus: Global Justice and Christian Lifestyle* (Maryknoll, N.Y.: Orbis Books, 1977), p. 98.

46. Quoted by Roger Shinn in a eulogy to Margaret Mead.

47. Benjamin A. Rogge, Speech before the Foundation on Economic Education, Oakland, Calif., September 24, 1979.

48. Reported in *San Francisco Chronicle,* May 16, 1979.

49. R. Buckminster Fuller, *Operating Manual for Spaceship Earth* (New York: Simon and Schuster, 1969), p. 59.

Bibliography

Alves, Rubem A. *A Theology of Human Hope.* Washington: Corpus Books, 1971.

Barney, Gerald O., ed. *The Unfinished Agenda: The Citizen's Policy Guide to Environmental Issues.* New York: Thomas Y. Crowell, 1977.

Bradford, Frederick A. *Money and Banking.* New York: Longmans, Green, 1938.

Browne, Harry. *You Can Profit from a Monetary Crisis.* New York: Macmillan Co., 1974.

Dewey, Edward R. *Cycles: The Science of Prediction.* New York: Holt, 1949. Reprint. New York: Manor Books, 1973.

Dusenberry, James S. *Money and Credit Impact and Control.* Englewood Cliffs, N.J.: Prentice-Hall, 1972.

Edwards, George C. *Money.* Berkeley: Wetzel, 1923.

Exter, John. "Money in Today's World." In *Champions of Freedom,* edited by Barbara Smith. Hillsdale, Mich.: Hillsdale College Press, 1975.

Finnerty, Adam D. *No More Plastic Jesus: Global Justice and Christian Lifestyle.* Maryknoll, N.Y.: Orbis Books, 1977.

Fremery, Robert de. "Banking Reforms to Stop Periodic Liquidity Crises." *The Commercial and Financial Chronicle,* July 9, 1970. See also issues for September 23, 1965, and July 20, 1967.

Fuller, R. Buckminster. *Operating Manual for Spaceship Earth.* New York: Simon and Schuster, 1969.

Galbraith, John Kenneth. *The Great Crash, 1929.* Boston: Houghton Mifflin, 1961.

Groseclose, Elgin. *Money: The Human Conflict.* Norman, Okla.: University of Oklahoma Press, 1934.

Handy, Robert T. "The American Religious Depression." *Church History,* March, 1960.

Heilbroner, Robert L. *Business Civilization in Decline.* New York: W.W. Norton, 1976.

————. *An Inquiry into the Human Prospect.* New York: W.W. Norton, 1974.

Jegan, Mary E., and Wilber, Charles K. *Growth with Equity.* New York: Paulist Press, 1979.

Kincheloe, Samuel C. *Research Memorandum on Religion in the Depression.* New York: Social Science Research Council, 1937.

Lappé, Frances Moore. *Diet for a Small Planet.* New York: Ballantine Books, 1975.

Lee, Robert. *Religion and Leisure in America: A Study in Four Dimensions.* New York: Abingdon Press, 1964.

————, and Casebier, Marjorie. *The Spouse Gap: Weathering the Marriage Crisis during Middlescence.* New York: Abingdon Press, 1971.

McGregor, Douglas. *The Human Side of Enterprise.* New York: McGraw-Hill, 1960.

Nisbet, Robert. *Twilight of Authority.* New York: Oxford University Press, 1975.

Oates, Wayne. *Confessions of a Workaholic: The Facts about Work Addiction.* New York: Abingdon Press, 1972.

Parsson, Jens O. *Dying of Money.* Boston: Wellspring Press, 1974.

Perry, Ralph Barton. *Puritanism and Democracy.* New York: Vanguard Press, 1944.

Rostow, W. W. *The Stages of Economic Growth: A Non-Communist Manifesto.* Cambridge: Cambridge University Press, 1960.

Rothbard, Murray. *America's Great Depression.* Princeton: Van Nostrand, 1963. Reprint. New York: Sheed and Ward, 1975.

Ruff, Howard J. *How to Prosper during the Coming Bad Years.* Alamo, Calif.: Target Publishers, 1978.

Schumacher, E. F. *Small Is Beautiful: Economics as if People Mattered.* New York: Harper & Row, 1973.

Shuman, James B., and Rosenau, David. *The Kondratieff Wave.* New York: World Publishing, 1972.

Sprinkel, Beryl W. *Money and Markets: A Monetarist View.* Homewood, Ill.: R. D. Irwin, 1971.

Terkel, Studs. *Working: People Talk About What They Do All Day and How They Feel About What They Do.* New York: Random House, Pantheon Books, 1974.

Tilden, Freeman. *World in Debt.* New York: Funk and Wagnalls, 1936.

White, Andrew Dickson. *Fiat Money Inflation in France.* Irvington-on-Hudson, N.Y.: The Foundation for Economic Education, 1959.

Wogaman, J. Philip. *The Great Economic Debate: An Ethical Analysis.* Philadelphia: Westminster Press, 1977.